TURNING POINTS 3

JASE SOUDER

Published by
Hybrid Global Publishing
333 E 14th Street
#3C
New York, NY 10003

Manufactured in the United States of America, or in the United Kingdom when distributed elsewhere.

Souder, Jase
Turning Points 3
     ISBN: 978-1-961757-85-1 softcover
     ISBN: 978-1-961757-86-8 ebook

Cover design by: Joe Potter
Copyediting by: Claudia Volkman
Interior design by: Suba Murugan

CONTENTS

CONTENTS

THREE STEPS TO BECOMING A SUCCESSFUL REAL ESTATE INVESTOR

Janice Bell, PhD

Most of us have a job, whether it's with a company or the government. We trade our time for money, and many times the decisions we face are made by someone else.

But what if you could have more money coming into your bank account? More control over the time you spend to make that money? More time to do what you want instead of trading your hours for dollars? Through owning your own business and/or investments, you can have control over those decisions.

I went from an overworked biotech employee to owning rental properties in five cities, and in two years I owned sixty units. Now I have money and time freedom. Would you like to learn how I did it?

I believe you can add real estate to your investing, whether active or passive. I believe you can recognize the behaviors that are keeping you in a job trading your time for money. I believe you can learn how to make strategic investing decisions that increase your wealth.

Are you looking to increase your cash flow so you can retire younger, healthier, and wealthier with *more time* for family, friends, and the activities you enjoy? If part of your wealth vision is to live in your purpose and have an impact in the world, this chapter is for you.

As I share my story, I want you to imagine how this would work for you too.

Right now, I run my own real estate investments, my schedule is mine, I have monthly cash flow, and I choose when to go on vacation with my family. I enjoy hiking, water sports, travel, educational seminars, and personal development conferences. This year I completed a high ropes course and learned how to eat fire! I volunteer my time training teenagers in Scouting and was able to spend a week teaching nature merit badges at a Scout summer camp in Oregon. My boss (aka me) said, "That's a great idea; you should go."

But my life wasn't always like this. Early in my career, I worked for several companies, from a start-up to a full production company. I was stuck in a nine-to-five biotech job with no joy or fulfillment. I was terrified to ask for a raise. I had a huge mortgage, full-time day care, and auto expenses. Making money was hard, and with the commute, I was gone eleven hours a day. I was away from family including baby twins and a high school student in sports. My husband and I were working offset hours just so one of us was home in early morning or before dinner.

I set goals to make more money or get promoted. Then company strategies would shift or my boss would change positions and I had to impress a new boss. I felt exhausted, overworked, and underappreciated.

And then, with a downturn in the stock market, the company laid off twenty-seven of us. I was devastated. Not only was my job gone, but those stock options they promised us were almost worthless.

I studied the real estate market with books, CDs and bootcamps. I began buying rental properties, and I quickly turned three condos into a large portfolio. In two years, through refinancing loans, creative financing, and 1031 exchanges, I turned those three condos into sixty units in five cites.

And that's why I'm writing this story…

I want you to discover the people and data you need to invest in real estate. I want you to overcome old habits and systematize your real estate business. I want you to transform into a leader of your own successful business with the time freedom to expand your life outside your job/career.

I discovered a three-step formula that helps create these outcomes for my clients: Discover, Systematize, and Transform.

DISCOVER THE PEOPLE AND DATA NEEDED

My coaching student Dave came to me after he bought his first rental duplex from an investor in another state. He found things were a mess. His property manager had no good contractors, no photo proofs of work completed, and no receipts. Every month, all Dave got was an invoice asking him to pay more money than the rent they had collected. He worked a demanding job and thought real estate was an investment and therefore passive. I coached him to ask for photos and receipts, and through this process, he discovered that 1) his property manager was cheating him, and 2) the city would not renew his landlord license until he fixed some major items.

Dave learned how to fire the property management company, discover new ones, manage people, ask the city inspector for clarity, negotiate with people for what he deserved, and manage a new contractor to do the repairs.

In my coaching, students learn to find the right *who*: the right realtors, contractors, and property managers. They develop negotiation skills and discover how to manage people, even if they never learned that in school.

Real estate investing is not just about the numbers—it's a people business.

To get started with real estate investing, you need to discover the right people and the right data to use in buying the property and managing it. You need to demand proof of all the work being done with your money.

SYSTEMATIZE AND STRUCTURE YOUR BUSINESS

Another coaching student, Sarah, was running her real estate investments with her boyfriend. They both worked full time and did the tasks for the business that they liked to do. The rest of the tasks? Well, they were falling through the cracks and not getting done. During our coaching, I had them organize a list of all the tasks into three buckets: marketing, finance, and operations. After they reviewed the list, they had to take ownership of a bucket or delegate it to a virtual assistant.

To structure your real estate investing, you must have systems like any business. When each partner is only doing the parts of the business they enjoy, the business is leaking time and/or money and no one sees it.

TRANSFORM YOURSELF INTO A SUCCESSFUL BUSINESS LEADER

Another coaching student had become friends with her tenants and listened to their stories about how broke they were. She was worried they would become homeless, and they took advantage of her by paying their rent late or not paying at all. Some tenants allowed relatives who were not on the lease to move in, and they caused damage to the property. She was discouraged and wanted to sell her units or just quit.

In our coaching sessions, we uncovered some childhood fears of homelessness that were causing her not to be objective. I taught her how to see her rentals as a business and remove herself as a friend. She began to rely more on her property manager. I led her to see that her job as a landlord was to provide a safe, clean place for tenants to live. If she thought they needed more help, she could always hire a social worker to visit the property. She began to see her defined role as the business owner and let her property manager handle the tenants.

Finally, let me tell you about John's results after completing my coaching program. When he came to me, he was a busy engineer with a passion for sports and travel. His rental was not paying him anything. It needed lots of repairs, the tenant was moving out, abandoned cars were accumulating in the front yard, and there was a government lien on the property. John was not sure what to do or even where to start. After coaching with me, John now has a remodeled property, a paying tenant, good property management, the lien removed, and he is looking for his next property. He has learned to negotiate one on one with sellers of off-market properties (in other words, no realtor involved), and he's gained confidence in his ability as a landlord and business owner.

Are you ready for a paradigm shift? Information is a necessary part of investing, and to be successful, you need a coach who has been where you are going and can point you in the right direction. I can teach you to apply my formula for success: Discover, Systematize, and Transform.

Janice Bell, PhD started her career with a PhD in Marine Biology, transitioned into the biotech industry, and then moved into full-time real estate investing. Janice hosts a monthly RE Club, mentoring private lenders and real estate investors on how to find and work with each other. She incorporates NLP with her RE knowledge.

wisewealthuniversity.com

THE PAIN THAT BINDS

Desi Bolin

The day I found out I was pregnant for the third time was one of those moments that forever split my life into a "before" and "after." The news came as a surprise, but it filled me with a sense of wonder and anticipation. I was about to embark on a journey that would redefine everything. But what unfolded was far from the story I had imagined.

Balancing the demands of a thriving business with the joy of expecting a child was exhilarating but also exhausting. My business was reaching new heights; we were hitting milestones I had only dreamed of when I started. Yet, amid the excitement, a relentless fatigue began to creep in. I felt as though I was constantly racing against time, trying to excel in every role I played.

In those early days of my pregnancy, I tried to do it all. I attended every meeting, answered every email, and took on every new challenge that came my way. I told myself I was strong enough—I could handle it all. But deep down, I was struggling physically and emotionally to keep up with the demands. The long hours, the stress, and the pressure I placed on myself all were taking a toll.

Then came the day when everything changed. A routine checkup quickly turned into a nightmare as I heard the devastating words from the doctor: "There's no heartbeat." In an instant, the future I had eagerly anticipated was shattered. The plans I had carefully crafted dissolved, leaving behind an emptiness that is impossible to articulate. The loss was profound, and it reverberated through every aspect of my life.

The days that followed were a blur of grief and confusion. I tried to make sense of what had happened, but there were no answers, no explanations that could fill the void. I felt lost, adrift in a sea of emotions I couldn't control. My thoughts were consumed with questions: *Why did this happen? Was it something I did? Could I have prevented it?* These questions haunted me, even though I knew rationally there was nothing I could have done.

In the aftermath, I attempted to dive back into work, hoping it would serve as a distraction. Work had always been my haven, a place where I could achieve, control, and feel a sense of accomplishment. But now, it felt different. The passion that once fueled me had dimmed, and my energy was depleted. I found myself going through the motions, but my heart wasn't in it.

As the days turned into weeks, the exhaustion deepened. What started as a lingering tiredness soon evolved into a pervasive sense of burnout. The motivation that had once driven me was nowhere to be found, and the spark that had ignited my creativity was gone. Even the simplest tasks became overwhelming. I was drained, not just physically, but emotionally and mentally as well.

My business, which had once been a source of pride, now felt like an insurmountable burden. I began to question everything: my decisions, my capabilities, and even the very foundation of what I had built. It seemed as though the loss had taken not just a piece of my heart, but also my confidence. The person staring back at me in the mirror each morning was a shadow of the woman who had once been so sure of her path.

There were moments when I considered walking away from it all. The thought of leaving behind the business I had worked so hard to build was heartbreaking, but so was the thought of continuing in the state I was in. I felt stuck, unable to move forward or backward, trapped in a cycle of grief and exhaustion.

My healing was not marked by a single revelation but by a series of small, deliberate steps. It began with accepting the pain, acknowledging the grief I had tried so hard to suppress. I realized that this loss was a part of my story and needed to be honored, not hidden away.

Seeking help was another crucial step, one I had long resisted in my driven, entrepreneurial mindset. Personal growth provided a space where I could untangle the complex emotions weighing me down. Speaking about the loss and the subsequent challenges allowed me to process the grief in ways I hadn't before. It was difficult but necessary.

I began to understand that my grief was not something to "get over"; it was something to integrate into my life. It wasn't a wound that would simply heal with time; it was a part of me, shaping who I was and who I would become. This realization was both painful and liberating. It allowed me to start rebuilding, not by trying to return to who I was before, but by embracing who I was now.

This period of reflection also led me to reassess my relationship with my business. I confronted some difficult questions: Why was I doing this? What did I want my business to represent? And how could I rebuild in a way that honored both my personal journey and my professional aspirations?

The answers didn't come all at once, but gradually a new vision began to take form. I wanted my business to be more than just a vehicle for success or financial gain. It had to reflect my values and serve as a platform for positive change.

I restructured the business, streamlining operations so I could focus on what truly mattered. Delegating tasks that were draining my energy allowed me to concentrate on areas where I could have the most impact. I also aligned the company's mission with my personal values, shifting our focus to initiatives that supported women and families. This was my way of turning pain into purpose, using my experience to help others who might be facing similar challenges.

One of the most important changes I made was to our company culture. I began to prioritize the well-being of my team, recognizing that burnout wasn't just something that happened to individuals; it was a systemic issue that needed to be addressed. We introduced more flexible work arrangements, encouraged time off, and made personal growth resources available to everyone. I wanted my team to feel supported, to know that their health and happiness mattered as much as their productivity.

Self-care became a nonnegotiable part of my routine. Mindfulness and meditation became essential tools for staying grounded, helping me maintain balance in both my personal life and my work. These practices were no longer luxuries but necessities for my well-being.

At first, these changes felt unfamiliar, even uncomfortable. I was so used to pushing myself to the limit that it was hard to slow down, to give myself permission to rest. But over time, I began to see the benefits. I started to feel more energized, more focused. The fog of exhaustion began to lift, and with it, the joy of running my business returned.

Looking back, I see that difficult period as a pivotal moment in my life and career. The experience of losing a pregnancy was devastating—an event that I would never wish on anyone. But it also forced me to reevaluate how I had been living and working, which led to profound changes.

Today, my business is not just performing well; it is built on a stronger foundation. We've created a culture that values well-being, understands the importance of balance, and prioritizes purpose over profit. We're more than just a company; we're a community of people passionate about making a difference.

The loss and the challenges that followed have brought clarity to my life. They taught me that life and business are not separate entities—they are intertwined.

The way we live our lives impacts how we run our businesses, and vice versa. Embracing this truth has allowed me to build something that is not just successful but deeply fulfilling.

As I continue to grow and evolve, both personally and professionally, I carry the lessons from that time with me. I now know the importance of slowing down, of taking a step back when necessary. I now know that the most difficult experiences can often lead to the most profound transformations.

The road ahead will undoubtedly present more challenges, but I face them with a renewed sense of purpose and resilience. My business is a testament to the strength that comes from enduring hardship and to the power of turning pain into progress.

That period of loss and exhaustion didn't break me. Instead it reshaped me, enabling me to rebuild a life and a business that align with who I am and what I believe in. And for that, I am both humbled and grateful.

This chapter in my life is not an ending—it's a turning point. It serves as a reminder that even in our darkest moments, there is potential for growth, healing, and new beginnings. And that is the legacy I choose to carry forward.

Desi Bolin is the founder and CEO of Virtually Sourced Solutions LLC, an international Virtual Executive™ consultancy firm with pillars of freedom, strength, support, stability, and security. As a published author, course creator, and certification founder, she and the team truly put their more than sixty specialties to highly efficient, highly effective use.

virtuallysourced.com

TURNING REJECTION INTO TRIUMPH: THE POWER OF PERSEVERANCE

Tatiana Bowers

To accomplish great things, we must not only act, but also dream; not only plan, but also believe.

—Anatole France

In 2007, my husband, son, and I moved from California to Oregon due to my husband retiring from a twenty-seven-year career in the Navy and getting a civilian job. I had earned my master's in counseling psychology in 2005 and was eager to start my new career. Being a licensed Marriage and Family Therapist with my own private practice had been my big dream for a long time.

This dream's seeds were sowed after going to therapy myself for childhood issues like bullying, learning disabilities, and other childhood trauma. I found therapy to be helpful, healing, and a great launching pad to living an authentically successful life. The seeds of my dream were nurtured when I sought out ways to help others that were hurting. This led me to being a volunteer rape crisis counselor, which came so naturally to me. It was such an honor and privilege to be with someone in so much pain and be able to be a safe space for them. The seeds of my dream germinated and started to grow when I was accepted into the master's program. School was hard but so fulfilling, and I felt like I was in the palm of God's hand.

After our move, I drove down to Salem, Oregon, to submit my application for my internship license as a Marriage and Family Therapist in person. When I asked when I could start practicing, they said "Right away." I couldn't wait!

Getting my internship license was one step closer to my dream. My heart was set on creating my own private practice. To do this I had to find a supervisor to validate the rest of three thousand hours I needed to get my full license, while needing to find an office to set up my practice. It all came together when I found an office and a supervisor in the same place. I offered free support groups to get my name out to the public and marketed myself through Psychology Today. For the next year, I focused on filling my private practice with clients and accumulating the hours for my full license.

Out of the blue, I received an email in mid-2008 from the Oregon State board of licensing for therapists and counselors. It was brief but devasting. The email said they did not approve my license. I was horrified. I felt like a complete and utter failure. The reason for the denial was that my educational credentials did not meet Oregon licensing requirements, even though these credentials had been accepted in California since I got my internship license there prior to our move.

I got together with my school's credentialing board, and they came to my rescue. They came out to Oregon and met with the Oregon board and stated our case. We walked out feeling pretty good that the outcome would be in our favor. A week went by, and once again the Oregon board let me know that they would not accept my school's accreditation. I was now out of luck. I would never be able to practice as a therapist in Oregon. I had done everything right, and this was the end of my dream. For me to get my license, we would have to move to another state, which wasn't feasible for our family. My heart was broken, and I was sad, discouraged, and depressed.

With this news, I had to close my office, say goodbye to my clients, and get a "JOB" that did not fulfill my dream. I felt defeated and hopeless. For the next three years, I worked as an adjunct professor for two colleges, teaching psychology, college success, and social issues and ethics. Meanwhile, our son was struggling in school and getting involved with the wrong crowd. This caused me to focus on figuring out how to help him.

Finally, around 2011, I started to try to figure out how to get my dream back in motion. Since we lived in the Portland, Oregon, area, I looked north of us to Washington State. I did research and found out that I met all the requirements for Washington State, so I applied for an internship license in Washington. They came back and said I needed one credit of Human Sexuality to get my internship license. After taking that class, I sent my transcript to Washington State.

Like magic, they mailed me my internship marriage and family license. It felt like redemption and a real step forward again toward my dream. The once-wilted plant of a dream was given new life.

Now that I had my internship license in Washington, we needed to move there. My husband found a great job just north of Seattle, and we settled into our new home. In order to get the rest of the three thousand hours required to get my license before opening my private practice, I got a job at a Community Mental Health Organization working with adults that were low-income. It was rewarding as well as a learning experience. Knowing I needed children and family hours as part of my licensing requirements, I changed jobs and got fired due to my lack of full participation in political discussions that were slanted to one political viewpoint. I walked out of that experience with my head held high knowing my work with my clients was truly impactful and made a difference in the lives of the children I served.

Even with this setback, my dream continued growing. My spouse supported my opening my own private practice, and in March 2016 I opened the doors of Embrace Hope Counseling. That summer, I acquired my additional hours for licensure by volunteering at a camp for foster kids and passed the national exam the first time around. Finally, at the end of September 2016, my full license arrived in the mail. It had been eight years since Oregon's rejection email. My dream had grown into a small tree with healthy leaves and was growing strong.

Embrace Hope Counseling has been a successful business and private practice for more than eight years. My clients have overcome devastating problems and issues to live vibrant and successful lives. Children have become free and confident young people. Marriages have been healed and made better. These things could never have happened if I had not taken all the steps needed to make my dream happen. My dream has become a strong tree and is producing fruit that will last a lifetime.

Don't miss your opportunity to make a difference in the world just because you have been told no! Find the way to take a step and say yes. The key tools I learned from this experience and have implemented in my life are as follows:

The grieving process is a real thing. Grief is not only when someone dies; it is also when dreams are denied and relationships end. There is no time limit for grief, so do not let anyone tell you when you "should" be over it. The stages of Grief are denial, anger, depression, bargaining, and acceptance. Be patient with yourself.

Learn what self-care looks like for you. Get good rest, eat good food, and take good care of yourself. Practice breathing, praying and meditating, exercising, and seek positive materials to read or listen to. I explored painting during this time.

After the grieving has faded, be kind and caring to yourself. You may suffer with triggers, so learn to recognize them and acknowledge that pain. Take one step at a time and don't rush yourself.

Try to find the things that are going well in your life. Start a gratitude journal. Seek the silver lining in any situation.

Look around you for your resources and support systems. Along the way, I have used self-help groups, therapy, friends, and many other resources. It takes courage and vulnerability to seek help and support. However, you do not know what will be given unless you ask. The worst thing might be another "no." And a "no" can turn into a yes or even a new possibility.

Each of us are made to live big and amazing lives that contribute to the world. Own your dreams, create goals to get to your dreams, and create action steps to get to those goals. Do not let situations or others stomp on your dreams, and if you hit a dead end, just back up and look for another way to reach your dream.

So many of our dreams at first seem impossible, then they seem improbable, and then, when we summon the will, they soon become inevitable.

—Christopher Reeve

Tatiana Bowers, MA, LMFT, is the founder of Embrace Hope Counseling and Authentic Success. Tatiana is passionate about getting people and businesses from simply surviving to thriving in amazing ways. She is a marriage and family therapist and business relationship facilitator, speaker, and author. Her motto is "You Are Amazing!"

www.embracehopecounseling.com

KEEP MOVING IN SPITE OF THE PAUSES

Aryana Charise

In my teens, I was determined to avoid the "freshman fifteen" in college. Although I ate whatever I wanted to eat, I also exercised regularly and walked daily to and from classes. I thought I had it all figured out, but when I hit thirty, I realized the game changed. I put on excess weight, my blood pressure increased, and my doctor told me I was prediabetic. I was tired all the time, and it seemed like whatever I ate caused me to gain weight. I found myself frustrated and disappointed. I was determined, though, to figure out the mystery once and for all so I could continue eating the foods I loved and still lose weight. It was an uphill battle that I refused to lose.

I sought the advice of doctors as well as friends who had been successful on the journey to achieve the best health possible. I knew I had to make some lifestyle changes, so I did. I joined a gym and started working out three to four times a week. I did a combination of cardio and resistance training, and I began seeing results. However, I still found myself coping with weight gain, bloating, sleeping challenges, and both mental and physical fatigue.

The turning point came while I was working in a call center for a beverage company assisting customers with questions and concerns. One day I got a call that surprised me. The caller asked, "How much sugar is in a can of soda?" I had no idea even though I was drinking three to five cans of soda daily. I politely replied, "I will be glad to check on that for you," and placed the caller on hold while I researched it. When I discovered the answer, I was shocked. I somehow had to tell her that there are twelve teaspoons of sugar in one can of soda. She thanked me for the information, and we hung up.

I sat in silence after that call and made a decision to cut back from drinking three to five sodas a day. I decided I would replace my consumption of soda with water. This was a challenge for me considering how much I loved soda and how much I did not care for water. I convinced myself that it was for the best. I needed help in doing this, so I played a game with myself. Since I was working in a call center, I decided that every time the phone rang, I would take a sip of water. Considering my phone rang two hundred times a day, this helped me drink more water. I am so glad I made this decision and discovered the many benefits of hydration, including increased energy, healthier skin, and weight loss.

I continued exercising and added more resistance training to my routine once I was in my forties. One of my friends invited me to a CrossFit gym. I was not familiar with this and decided to go to check it out. When I arrived, I was amazed at the exercises the participants were engaging in and wondered if this was a good fit for me. I was invited to stay for a workout, and I said, "Sure." I attempted to do the WOD (workout of the day) and found myself challenged by every exercise. I did exercises I never thought my body could do—pushups, squats with weights, running with sandbags on the back, burpees . . . oh my! I was done after one workout, and every muscle in my body was screaming. I walked out of that gym and headed straight to the grocery store to get the largest bag of Epsom salt I could find to soak and heal my body.

To my surprise, I slept soundly that night, and I decided to go back again and again to the CrossFit gym. I enjoyed the challenge and the way my body was adapting to the exercises. I learned how to push past limitations in the gym—and also in life. I continued this for five years, and during that time I realized the many benefits of exercising consistently with the support of others holding me accountable. I realized the power of having a coach, someone who pushes me to be my very best.

When COVID-19 hit and the gym closed, I was disappointed. I waited patiently for it and everything else to reopen. This led me to figure out how to exercise on my own. I was challenged during this time and found myself slacking off and being inconsistent with my exercise regimen. Once again I experienced gaining excess weight, bloating, sleeping challenges, mood swings, and high blood pressure. I now had high cholesterol and was again prediabetic. I was dehydrated, frustrated, and forty pounds overweight. In addition, I was experiencing symptoms of menopause. It started with perimenopause symptoms of irregular periods and some months no period at all. I experienced hot flashes and night sweats.

I reached out to my friends to find out what was happening. One of my friends, who was in her fifties told me, "Welcome to menopause!" I was not enjoying this at all, so I started researching how to cope with all these uncomfortable symptoms. It helped to know I was not the only one and that this was normal for women to experience. Yet I was determined to find out what I could do to alleviate the discomfort. I reached out for support from other women who were going through similar situations as well as those who were on the other side of it.

I researched natural remedies and began making lifestyle changes. I increased my water intake and eliminated my consumption of caffeine. I was advised to dress in layers to provide relief as I encountered fluctuating body temperatures. I learned to do Kegel exercises to strengthen my pelvic floor to prevent urinary incontinence. I got a kettlebell and used it for resistance training in addition to doing squats, planks, and pushups. I discovered the power of cooling pillows. I made dietary changes including adding herbal supplements and teas for relief. I hiked daily and also invested in an eighteen-speed bicycle. I found healing outside in nature swimming, kayaking, and walking. When the gym reopened, I returned; however, I kept the outdoor exercises as well walking in the morning or on breaks at work.

After making it through many sleepless nights, I decided to continue my education and research. I have shared my findings with women all over the world and helped them understand the hormonal changes and what can be done to get relief from the symptoms of perimenopause and menopause. While perimenopause can occur as early as age thirty-five, menopause typically begins between the ages of forty-five and fifty-five. Each woman's journey varies, and so do the symptoms she may encounter.

During these "pauses," eggs are released less frequently, which causes irregular menstrual cycles. It is beneficial to work with a holistic health practitioner in developing a plan to alleviate symptoms such as fatigue, headaches, night sweats, hot flashes, mood swings, and weight gain. It is my goal for women to overcome these challenges and then shine the light for other women to follow. Out of my journey has emerged the ability to help other women prevent and alleviate the pain and discomfort I experienced.

If you're experiencing these uncomfortable "pauses," know that you, too, can find joy in the journey!

Aryana Charise is a wellness coach, international speaker, and bestselling author of the book Harmonic Healing. She has a bachelor's degree in biology from Emory University in Atlanta, Georgia. Aryana specializes in educating and empowering women aged forty and older to achieve optimal health and well-being.

linkedin.com/in/aryanacharise

HOW THE GAME OF GOLF SAVED MY LIFE

Lori Danecke

How many of you reading this have ever felt lost and alone in a relationship?

How many of you reading this have ever done what was expected of you even though you didn't want to do it?

I know I have—and did and for most of my life!

I graduated high school, went to university, got married, bought a house, and had kids. These were the normal and expected things I was taught to do, so I did them. Don't get me wrong—I love my two boys, my daughters-in-law, and my four grandkids. I wouldn't trade them for the world. And it all came at the cost of losing myself in the process.

My now ex-husband was a kind and gentle man (otherwise I never would have married him). While all the clues were there before we got married, though, I chose, unconsciously, to ignore them.

Conversations we had were without depth, short, and infrequent as time passed. I felt alone, rejected, unheard, unseen, and unloved. This created a lot of anger that was eating me alive. The best way to describe it is that when I was home by myself, I felt alone, angry, and scared. When my husband was home, I felt lonely, sad, and hurt! There was little to no affection. We were able to put up the front of being a happy couple when with family and friends.

The longer I stayed, the worse I felt about myself—to the point where I hated who I was and what I had become. I was living a lie and didn't see a way out without hurting anyone. I betrayed myself in so many ways, and this resulted in a deep depression.

I chose to stay for nearly thirty-five years because I had no confidence in myself and felt stuck where I was.

I love the game of golf, and that became my refuge. I played as often as I could. It was one of the few places I felt I could be myself. Then my home life began to invade my golf life, and I carried the anger and resentment to the course. I became the angry, frustrated club-slamming, cussing golfer. I wasn't having fun anymore, and I'm sure my golf partners weren't having much fun playing with me either.

Then I came across an opportunity that changed everything for me. I took a five-day class centered on the golf mindset because I had a goal of winning the club championship. I learned several tools that helped change my game, and I dedicated myself to practice not only the skills of the game but the skills of the mind. I learned that the game of golf is 90 percent mindset and 10 percent skill.

The more I implemented these tools, the better I felt, and it became the springboard for real change for me. The game of golf saved my life!

I won that championship, and the rest is history! My entire life changed. As I became more confident and had more belief in myself, I continued to change and come to the realization that I deserved more.

I worked with the coach who put on that class to dig into where all the lack of belief in myself started, and I released a lot of negative thoughts, beliefs, and emotions that were holding me hostage in all areas of my life. Through this process, I discovered a part of me I had buried for decades. I found a confident, self-assured woman, secure in who she was and where she wanted to go!

There was a moment of brief hesitation before I made a bold move: I made the decision to put myself first, knowing it was not only the best decision for me but also for everyone else involved.

Yes, I was nervous and a little scared. I knew that I deserved to live the life I wanted and do what was best for me. It was actually the most selfless thing I had ever done. I was tired and exhausted from doing everything for everyone else, so on February 2, 2022, I asked for what I wanted—a DIVORCE!

I had packed my car and was ready to go, there was nothing to say that would change my mind. All that was left was to have what could be a difficult conversation.

Once I took that last deep breath, I said what I needed to say with a self-assuredness I hadn't experienced in a very long time. I did feel badly for my husband, yet I stuck to what I knew was the right decision and action for me. I felt empowered to put myself first and secure that I had made the right decision for me.

Seven weeks after I left, I purchased an RV that I had dreamt about for two years, and I fulfilled my vision of traveling around Canada and the United States on my own!

I have created the life I desire and deserve. I have my sense of adventure and wonderment back. I have been to parts of the world I never thought were possible, including Kenya for a golf safari and Spain for an LPGA golf event, with more to come. I have met people I never would have the pleasure of experiencing if I had stayed stuck.

My whole experience since then has been one of growth and change. I'm a completely different person now. I'm living where I dreamt about since I was twelve. My relationships with the people in my life are so much better than they ever were before because the relationship I have with myself is the best it has ever been.

I will continue to grow. It's not always going to be easy, and it'll be worth every second. I've gone from doubt to confidence, from hating myself to loving myself, from hiding and being scared to being bold and self-assured. I can hardly wait to experience what life has in store for me next. I'm ready.

And remember this: No matter how old you are: IT'S NEVER TOO LATE!

Lori Danecke is a master certified practitioner and coach in NLP, quantum release process, hypnotherapy, and Reiki. The proud mom of two boys and four grandkids, she is a lifelong learner who loves to travel the world and discover new places and treasures.

linkedin.com/in/lori-danecke-a63811234/

ATTRACT YOUR SOULMATE IN SEVEN SECONDS

Patricia Fuqua

Recently I celebrated my sixteenth year of supporting hundreds of people in the United States to move from loneliness to lasting love.

I've published two books on how readers can find and keep the love of their life so they can build beautiful memories together. I've hosted a TV show sharing spiritual tips for living your best life. I'm married to the love of my life, and we have three wonderful daughters and three adorable grandsons.

I awaken to the birds singing sweetly outside my upstairs window. Before I open my eyes, I listen for the soft breathing of the man of my dreams next to me and put my hand on his chest. He pulls me close. His warmth enfolds me, and I feel cherished.

This has been our morning ritual for the past fifty years.

But it wasn't always this way.

For years, as an ambitious professional woman, I dated without a purpose. I started to feel lonely because there was an emptiness to going out on endless dinners with strangers I didn't care about, and I blamed them for being underwhelming.

It all changed when a roommate invited me to a party after informing me that my life was too boring. She declared I needed some fun. I agreed.

When I got there, a buzz of excitement started in my tummy. There were more men than women, and they all were well-dressed and educated. I formulated a plan for the evening—I'd network around the room, and if I hadn't met someone special before I reached the front door, I'd slip out the front door and go home.

As I chatted with one man, a soldier, I felt someone looking at me. I turned and looked into the dark eyes of a handsome man and thought, *There's my husband.* I continued conversing with the soldier until the stranger asked me to dance. When our hands, touched a spark flew up my arm and landed in my heart. My brain said, *YEP, it's my husband. This feels like home.*

We were inseparable for the rest of the evening. We chatted and danced. He left my side to give his grandmother a ride home and asked me to stay until he returned. I told him I would if he returned within the hour. He did.

He asked me out to a movie the following Saturday.

That was the beginning of our date nights over the decades, making beautiful memories, including vacations at five-star resorts, backyard gatherings with friends and family, and quiet moments on the couch together.

Contained in that first meeting is the powerful system I now use to support hundreds of men and women to find and keep the partner of their dreams. My coaching works because I believe you can find your partner, and I believe you can keep your partner. You can enjoy an amazing, lasting love relationship while making beautiful memories.

That's why I do what I do.

I've taken a lot of classes on mediation, meditation, and the law of vibration and combined them into a system that provides a practical dating strategy combined with mental housekeeping and values clarification.

My system works because clients raise their standards and keep their minds focused on their dating goal while increasing their self-awareness and self-care.

But enough about me. Would you like to hear about the three stepping stones I use to help my clients attract and keep the love of their life?

It starts with a personality and energetic assessment. From there, the first stepping stone is mental housekeeping. Clients learn to manage what they are thinking about self, the opposite sex, and relationships. Most of you may not be aware of the negative story you tell yourself that keeps you alone and miserable. This story needs to be replaced with positive thoughts that move you toward your relationship goal. Self-defeating thoughts like "There are no good men left for me" will kill the possibility of finding your relationship match.

A woman who had been alone for twenty years contacted me. She left a relationship with a man who had commitment issues and didn't want to marry after they lived together for five years. She generalized bitterly that no man would want a lasting love relationship. She refused to correct her limited thinking and doomed herself to remain bitter and resentfully alone.

In contrast, when my roommate suggested that a party would cheer me up, I grabbed the opportunity. I was ready to move to an amazing love relationship. I was done with loneliness and open to a new result.

My magical transformation from thinking my dates were underwhelming to expecting I would find one exciting guy who would become my husband made all the difference in my experience at that party.

Another client had been alone for sixteen years and was convinced that all the good men were married to her friends. I helped her shift her thinking to believing there was one good man for her, and it was her job to find him. She was married in twelve months.

Thoughts are things that we use to raise our vibrations so we can have more of what we desire. When we focus on the possibilities that we want, we automatically raise our vibration and inevitably increase our ability to find the soulmate we seek.

The second stepping stone is creating a clear vision of what you desire. It needs to be detailed and contain the primary feeling you want to experience with your soulmate.

One of my clients wanted a partner who would travel to world-class ski resorts with her. He didn't have to ski, but he would be willing to have her favorite beverage and a hot bath with rose petals ready when she returned to the lodge after skiing. Her detailed vision brought her several suitors who were willing to answer her call to action.

My own clarified vision included sharing integrity, ambition, and family values with my partner. My guy showed me these qualities on the first meeting. He gave his grandmother a ride home and returned to the party when he said he would. I discovered his ambition as we dated.

Sarah had divorced twice, ending two marriages that made her miserable. She completed the exercises in my book *Manifest Your Soulmate* and soon met Elias online.

On their first date, they were completing each other's sentences and feeling like they'd won the lottery. He wanted to marry her the next weekend, but she said, "No, let's wait a bit." They met in November and married in February. She emailed me to say she finally felt respected, cherished, and loved.

Her vision of what she wanted to experience set her attraction of her right husband in motion. To get clear about what and who you want to experience in a lasting love relationship creates a powerful focus for your dating. Having a coach who holds you accountable ensures that you avoid settling for the kind of guy you know is wrong for you.

The third essential stepping stone is creating a personal effective dating strategy. In today's world, when a relationship-minded woman or man is looking for a life partner with whom to build beautiful memories, online dating apps offer increasing possibilities because each of them target a particular audience. Relationship-minded entrepreneurs and professionals have several to choose from.

To use dating apps effectively is a must. Too many women open a dating account and get no hits or just get a lot of hellos from unsuitable men. When a woman or man creates their online dating profile, it's important that they manage the all-important first impression. It takes only seven seconds to attract the right person to want to know more.

A man sat near me in an elegant little French restaurant one summer afternoon. He was dressed shabbily for that place, and I watched as on the spur of the moment he invited a woman to have a drink with him. I shuddered inwardly.

Elegantly dressed in denim and linen, she looked at him from the doorway, turned up her nose, and approached him slowly. She turned down his invitation to sit, saying she'd rather go shopping down the street before exiting. I struck up a conversation with him and helped him to see the importance of those initial seven seconds.

If you're open to learning how to find and keep the partner of your dreams, know that there are specific, simple strategies to set this in motion. Get ready to build beautiful memories!

Patricia Fuqua, Dating Queen for Amazing Lasting Love Relationships, is a bestselling author. She helps professionals and entrepreneurs who are skillful at making money but lack relationship skills. Using her proven and powerful system, she shows them how to find and keep the true love of their dreams so they can build beautiful memories together.

datingqueen.love

LOVE AND FORGIVENESS MAKE THE DIFFERENCE

Jeanell Greene

I never thought in a million years that my marriage would end in divorce. I grew up with loving parents who were great role models and showed me what real partnership, teamwork, and forgiveness looked like and how much fun it could be.

It was a whirlwind romance when I met my first husband, Rene. We fell in love hard and fast. We had so much fun traveling, boating, and living a comfortable life. And even though I noticed a lot of red flags, he checked all the boxes.

The proposal came in a matter of just a few months, and I was so excited that I would finally complete my role in the world as a wife and hopefully one day a mother.

My dad had just passed away a couple of months before I met Rene, and I was longing for a male figure in my life to keep me safe now that my dad was no longer around. It all seemed to make logical sense.

Everything was great . . . until we got home from our honeymoon.

The week after we got back, everything changed—*he* changed. It was like he was a totally different person, as though he had been wearing a mask. It was like he had just checked the "get married" box and now that it was fulfilled, he checked out.

He stopped going to church, going to family functions . . . and he even stopped showering.

More than anything, I felt so lonely. There I was, a young bride, all alone: eating alone, sitting on the couch alone, and going to church alone while my husband was doing his own thing. He was usually out with his friends fishing, in the garage building something, or working on his own personal projects.

I had no one to talk to. So many people had warned me about our quick engagement, and I had assured them I knew what I was doing, so how could I admit to them now that I had made a mistake? And so I kept it locked inside and did my best to put on a brave face. But deep down, I felt betrayed, duped, angry, and panicked. I had been dreaming of this moment in my entire life, when I would finally feel complete with my partner in crime. Instead, I was dreading the future with this person who often acted like a spoiled, rebellious teenage boy.

I also worried about what my mom would say if I decided to leave him. I remember lying in bed one night, staring at the ceiling, thinking and praying, *God, is this it? Is this what my life is going to be forever?* I became bitter, resentful, and mean. I started to become someone I didn't like. I felt unattractive, unheard, unappreciated, and unworthy. I started to change—and not for the better.

As a last attempt to fix our relationship, we met with a couples therapist, but my husband was unwilling to meet me halfway and take ownership for his part.

Then I heard about a weekend seminar called the Landmark Forum, which was designed to cause personal breakthroughs. We both signed up, and I thought to myself, *Great! Now he can go get himself fixed.*

But as the course progressed, I started to realize that this was more about ME than it was about him! For once, I took the focus off him and what he was (and wasn't) doing.

I saw that I had been blaming him and judging him, and because of my frustration, I was cold and mean. I saw that I had been trying to fix him and change him into someone he wasn't. I had expectations that he simply could not or would not fulfill, and I used that as an excuse to withhold my love. I had been so afraid of being alone, because deep down, I felt unworthy and unloved. I also recognized that I had real trust issues.

And so I sat down with Rene and apologized: "I'm so sorry for judging and blaming you. I'm sorry for trying to fix you and change you. I haven't taken responsibility for my expectations. You're perfect just the way you are—*and* you're not for me."

We decided to split up, and we even went to the law courts together. I came to the realization that I was the common denominator in all my failed relationships, and the Landmark course inspired me to do some digging to get to the source of these emotions, thoughts, and fears.

Then it hit me: All my trust issues and feelings of being unloved came from what happened to me when I was nine years old.

I was sitting on my bed when my mom called out to me and my siblings. Something in her voice told me something was wrong. We walked into the living room, and I saw my mom and dad standing by the front door, and beside my dad were brown leather luggage suitcases.

My mom then announced, "Kids, your dad is leaving. He doesn't love us anymore." And without a word, my dad left.

I stood at the bay window crying as I watched my dad go down our front steps and get into a brown car I didn't recognize. I remember feeling confused, shocked, sad, and terrified.

What I didn't know was that my dad was having an affair with another woman, who happened to be my mom's best friend. He had gotten her pregnant, and he had to make a choice: us or her. He chose her.

The next three years were a blur. I barely saw my dad during this time as my parents were going through the separation process. I often felt unsafe, alone, and scared. I had so many mixed emotions.

I was really angry with my dad, yet I had always been "Daddy's little girl," so I constantly felt torn and conflicted. I remember my dad dropping by my school one day just so he could see me. He had brought McDonald's for lunch as a sort of bribe, but I ran into the girls' bathroom, crying uncontrollably. I felt so disappointed and angry—but also so alone and scared.

And then one day, my dad came home. He went to my mom and said, "I'm sick. I need someone to take care of me. Can I come home?"

My mom said yes and decided to forgive him. From that moment forward, she never brought it up again.

She decided to make the SHIFT from being angry and sad to being loving and forgiving. Because she was committed to being a family and to her children growing up with a dad.

Three years later we got the call we were waiting for, and my dad went into surgery for his organ transplant.

The next extra thirteen years he got back were great. He became a better father and husband.

We went back to being a happy, connected family, and when he passed away at the age of fifty-three, we were all there—loving him, praying for him, and watching him pass peacefully.

Love and forgiveness saved my family that day. I learned that anything is possible when you have faith and hope.

And that's how my journey to self-growth and healing became my obsession . . . and then my life purpose in the pursuit of happiness and love for all mankind.

Here's an exercise you can use to move forward on your own journey:

> I learned that (fill in the blank) and it's my mission to share it.

> So I can (fill in the blank).

> So I don't have to (fill in the blank)

> So I can make a difference with (name community or people).

Remember:

1. You must come from the energy of love, not fear in order to experience true happiness.
2. Love and happiness are not possible without forgiveness. Forgiveness means you don't have to go another day holding on to the past, old grudges, or misunderstandings. Forgiveness allows you to let go of the hurt and suffering.
3. Forgiveness starts with forgiving yourself so you can then forgive others.
4. The more you understand who you are, and why you are the way you are, the more you can learn to have compassion and for yourself and others.

Don't waste your time on this earth holding resentment in your heart for something someone did long ago, thus missing out on opportunities to feel love, connection, and joy. Stop punishing yourself and others; stop feeling guilt, shame, and regret so you can finally have the beautiful family life you deserve, where everyone is happy, healthy, thriving, and feels truly seen, heard, valued and has a sense of belonging. With love and forgiveness, you can be the role model you've always wanted to be for your kids, your friends, and your community.

Jeanell Greene is a relationship coach and marriage expert known for saving countless marriages from infidelity and divorce while also addressing generational trauma. Her passion lies in rekindling the "best friend" dynamic for couples, allowing them to rediscover profound peace, forgiveness, and fun again.

IGNITING THE JOY WITHIN: A JOURNEY FROM DARKNESS TO A JOY-LED LIFE

Jan Hoath

I believe JOY is your birthright and greatest renewable resource. It's available to you at all times when you know how to access it.

I believe JOY is your soul superpower and unfair competitive advantage as a leader.

I believe JOY is your fastest, most fulfilling path to live and lead your legacy now.

I am an international speaker, bestselling author, poet, joy-filled leadership mentor, certified mindfulness meditation teacher, and I love helping successful women leaders create their joy-filled legacy as I get to live mine!

How great my life is now . . .

I love my life! I'm living in my dream home, a cozy cabin in the woods in the mountains with my yummy family of an Australian husband, two kids, a Bernese mountain dog and a fiercely independent cat, where I get to adventure in skiing, snowboarding, trail running and indulge in my other interests—surfing, sailing, learning to play the banjo, and kitchen dancing.

But it wasn't always this way . . .

The world felt dark and cruel. I felt utterly alone, as though no one could possibly understand me. I was left wondering what all of this was for—what life was about. I pondered deeply if I wanted to exit this life.

When the doctors told me that my career as a competitive swimmer was over, I was devastated. At the young age of fourteen, all I knew was that I wanted to be a world-class swimmer, just like my big sister. Yet there I stood, hearing the news that even after major reconstructive surgery on my shoulder, my body was simply not built for swimming at this level. I didn't know what to do with myself.

Have you ever lost an identity? A role that shaped how you showed up in the world?

My family and friends tried to comfort me in every way they could, but they didn't understand the depths of my sadness. I didn't know who I was supposed to be now. Without swimming, I felt like I didn't fit in anywhere—not even with my own family. Depression took hold, and I became a stranger in my own life.

My parents did what they thought was best. They sent me to therapy and put me on antidepressants. But I hated those "happy pills." Even at fourteen, I knew that trying to fix something from the outside wouldn't work. What I needed wasn't just a fix—I needed a complete transformation, something from deep within.

Have you ever felt like the solution offered to you didn't address what was truly going on inside?

At my lowest point, I was simply going through the motions of my teenage life, when one day, in German class, something happened that would change everything. My favorite substitute teacher, Frau Newman, called me over after class.

"Gabby!" she said with warmth in her voice, using my German nickname. She pulled me into the back room and pointed to a poster. It was an opportunity to be an exchange student in Germany. With a hunch that this could be my path forward, she told me about the program. In that moment, a tiny spark ignited inside of me—a little flicker of life I hadn't felt in months.

That was the first moment I felt joy again.

Do you remember the first time you felt a spark of hope after a time of darkness?

The mere thought of traveling to a foreign country, with new people, food, and experiences, felt like freedom. It gave me hope—something I hadn't felt in what seemed like forever.

I was so very appreciative of this unexpected angel in my life in the form of Frau Newman. And yet, as I consider this now, I realize that with any awakening or opening of a new path, new ideas and opportunities often come in the form of something unexpected.

Is there a moment in your life where something unexpected became the turning point you needed?

One joyful step at a time, I threw myself into that exchange student application, pouring my heart into every essay. When I was invited for an interview, I shared my story and my heart. That joy must have shone through because I was awarded one of only two scholarships offered in my state. It was the first moment I truly believed in a future filled with possibility.

Before I left, my family and therapist sat down to discuss my antidepressants. Knowing I was about to embark on a new adventure, far away from home and without the conveniences of modern communication, we all agreed it was time for me to stop taking the pills. With my therapist's blessing, I was free of them for good—and I've never needed them since.

I can now peacefully say that was a turning point, and I remain grateful for the support during my darkest days. But it was joy, not medicine, that was the true remedy for my spirit.

What has been the true remedy for your spirit in your darkest moments?

In Germany, I embraced my new identity fully. I allowed myself to experience everything—new people, new food, and new places—with wide-eyed wonder. I followed my joy, wherever it led me. This became a practice, a way of living, and eventually a philosophy I now call the joy-led life.

How often do you let joy guide your decisions?

That decision to live joyfully has taken me on the most magical, divine path. And it's a path I could never have premeditated or manufactured, no matter how hard I tried. Thinking my way out of my circumstance—my deep depression—was not what was going to transform my life.

Have you ever noticed how thinking your way through a problem doesn't always lead to the solution, but feeling your way through does?

Following my joy led me on an unconventional, uncharted path. From turning down a fantastic corporate job opportunity in Germany to moving to Aspen to become a world-class ski instructor, and then following my joy all the way to Australia, where I met my husband in the snow and with whom I eventually became the mother of two beautiful children.

Does your joy often lead you to places you never expected to go?

While my journey started at fourteen, that first spiritual awakening never left me. It was the profound moment when I realized that joy was my true medicine and my superpower in navigating life's challenges. It allowed me to triumph through adversity, come out stronger and wiser, and yes, more joyful.

I fondly recall Frau Newman being that unexpected angel in my life who really saw me, understood me, and could help me see a new inspiring way forward out of my darkness. Her perspective was broader than mine and one of hope and joy.

Have you had teachers, mentors, or others in your life who inspired you in unimaginable ways?

I knew early on—not that long after my year in Germany, actually—that I had a gift to really see others and help them find their most inspiring path forward.

For the last sixteen years, I've made it my mission not only to live a joy-led life but also to coach, mentor, and guide other women leaders to embrace their sacred superpower of joy. Together, we build lives without regret and create legacies of inspiration.

When we lead with joy, we automatically create a ripple effect—a radiant, infinite impact on the world around us.

How might your life change if you committed to leading with joy?

As you read this, I hope you feel inspired to pursue the joy in your own heart and witness the magic that unfolds when you, too, lead with joy. Embracing the journey of a joy-led life often requires guidance—someone who sees your potential, understands your struggles, and helps illuminate your path forward.

Who in your life could serve as that "angel" guide or mentor to help you fully embrace and live out your joy-led life?

The right guide can offer invaluable support, perspective, and encouragement as you navigate your unique journey. They can help you uncover and harness your inner joy, transforming challenges into opportunities and leading you toward a life filled with purpose and fulfillment. You deserve to live and lead a full, joy-filled life.

Seek out those who can help you discover and amplify the joy within you. Together, you can create a ripple effect that not only enhances your life but also inspires others to follow their own joy.

Are you ready to take the next step in your journey with the support of a guide who will help you unlock and live your fullest, joy-led life?

JOY Up.

 **Jan Hoath** is an international speaker and bestselling author. A leadership coach, mindfulness meditation teacher, former professional alpine ski instructor, and masterful student of life, she guides her clients to claim JOY as their superpower and find deep fulfillment leading with heart, no matter what challenges life brings.

janhoath.com

YOU ARE ALWAYS CREATING SOMETHING, SO LET'S CREATE SOMETHING MAGICAL!

Cindy Ju

I believe we all have the right to be seen, heard, and loved.

I believe each one of us has our own unique gifts that will make a big impact in the world.

I believe it all starts with being who you truly are and loving all parts of you for a happier, healthier, wealthier life.

I truly love my life right now. I have amazing relationships, both personally and professionally. I've been able to travel anytime I want, booking last minute flights, and even going to Thailand for a month every year for some "me time." I've designed my own line of merch, self-published a children's book and courses online, lost thirty pounds, gone private island hopping, and tried hang-gliding and ziplining, even with my fear of heights. One of the best things I've been able to give myself is multiple retirement, savings, and investments accounts—all while working from my she shed and around the world.

The grandest gift I've given myself is having the time to go back to school to get my certification on early childhood education and mental health wellness to be the best mom to my two boys and instill in them autonomy and full trust in their own intuition. I gave them a head start of what took me years and years to learn.

I've embraced all parts of me, and I truly love getting paid for being me. I love waking up every day and seeing how much love and fun I can bring to myself and the people in my life and my community worldwide.

But it always wasn't this way.

I was burned out and overworked and so tired of it. As a firstborn Asian American female immigrant, the value of hard work and being responsible was instilled in me. No one talked about the unspoken rules of putting yourself last and not speaking up for your own needs or happiness, so how could I? Neither I nor my parents were ever taught that. Honestly, I also hated myself because I was obese, depressed, and just surviving.

Then within a month of me "achieving" the American dream, everything fell apart. I had to sell my home at a $100K loss, and I had so much anxiety that I had to quit my six-figure job. I went into an even deeper, darker depression for five years. During that time I addressed years of things I'd suppressed, such as physical, emotional, and sexual abuse, abandonment, and self-worthiness. Just as a line from *Crazy Rich Asians*, I saw myself as a "poor, raised by a single mom, low-class, immigrant nobody."

I even believed that since I couldn't work anymore, I had no real value. I woke up every day tired and lonely—and to be honest, I didn't want to live anymore.

Do you know what that feels like? Do you know what it's like to feel unhappy and tired for so long that you don't even know where to begin and what to do? What was fun anymore? What was happy anymore? All I knew was trying to survive.

And then, one night as I lay awake at 3:00 a.m., something in me just said, *Don't keep thinking about dying—think about how to be okay and happy again.* So I googled "why am I not happy?" and that started a self-healing journey. I began asking myself some painful questions. I watched a ton of YouTube videos from spiritual leaders such as Oprah, Brené Brown, and Abraham-Hicks. I read many self-help books and began investing in myself to become the person I was seeking. I had suffered enough and now it was time to make a change.

And then I found the secret to regulate my intense emotions and add light and love from an energetic level: energy clearing. It was like I could finally breathe again, and it was a game changer that aligned my heart, mind, body, and soul instantly.

I found that energy clearing is a way to get to the root of the unconscious limiting beliefs that block us from really going for what we want and harness our true power, which allows that abundant life to flow to you. We pick up these beliefs, thoughts, and stories (or BTS as I call them) from our childhood, environment, and generational trauma, intentionally and unintentionally.

I have found that energy clearing is the fastest, easiest, and safest way to remove energetic blocks so you can be aligned with your heart, mind, soul and body for a happy, healthy, and wealthy life. I've seen miraculous and magical things happen not only for myself, but for others around me. Using energy clearing and reprogramming the mind allows real, lasting change to be embodied within you.

I've been able to do everything I've wanted to do, and now I get to dream even bigger and not only make my own dreams a reality, but also help other people in their life and business. And that's what I want for you, too: money in the bank; more than enough to spend on trips and courses or coaching or hobbies you want without hesitation; time to work out or volunteer and be creative with your life and time. Whatever kind of life you want, it is possible. You are already creating it, so why not create something magical?

The best is yet to come.

You have a God, the Universe, and divine gifts and talents for you to discover, harness, and share with the world. We need you. We need your stories. We need your love. We need you to show up for yourself and step into leadership so we all can learn faster and easier together. Do you feel the calling inside you? That deep desire will rot inside you or be set free to become the "YOU" you're meant to be. The real, authentic, loving, abundant being that you are.

Remember, be the change you want to see in the world. It starts with loving all parts of you.

Cindy Ju is a speaker, intuitive life coach, artist, published author, early childhood education teacher, and a thankful member of the universe. She has helped heart-centered, ambitious professionals align with their true power in life and business and go to the next level in love and abundance.

energyofbeingyou.com

TURNING TO FAITH

Natalie Lavelock

As I sat at my desk in Nursing Administration, staring at the skylight, trying to feel the calming warmth of that single ray of light descending into my office, I could feel the conflict arising within. It was an unsettled stirring that seemed to be signaling a change on the horizon. At first I didn't understand. What was God trying to tell me? I mean, by all external measures I had it all. I was near the top of the corporate ladder. I had the trust and respect of both the hospital administrators and my colleagues who worked at the bedside. What was there to change?

Have you ever felt that way? Have you ever felt, deep in your soul, that something big was about to happen, but you didn't know when or why?

As the feeling persisted, I started exploring other ways I could create even more impact within the organization through the programs and trainings I was creating and implementing. In doing so, I began exploring the world of coaching. I decided to take a course so that I could be a better trainer for the organization and create better programs for our patients. The course took about four months to complete, and I was excited to implement what I had learned!

Toward the end of my training, both the hospital CEO and the Chief Nursing Officer (CNO) decided to retire. They were an incredible team to work with and Lynne, my CNO, was not only an exceptional leader, but had become a mentor to me over the past couple of years. So when they announced their retirement, I was both elated for them and heartbroken for me. This must have been what I felt coming those several months ago.

Wrong!

Shortly thereafter, the new CNO was hired, and within just a couple of weeks my boss said she wanted to have a meeting. No big deal; we had regular meetings all the time. It was no secret she was hoping I would take her position as the Director of Women's Services for the hospital when she retired.

But on that day, her whole demeanor was different. As she walked into my office and sat down next to me, I could see the distress on her face. She sat down and said, "I have something I have to tell you and I hope you'll consider my offer."

Wait . . . what? What are you telling me, and what offer?

She proceeded to tell me that the new CNO had decided to eliminate my role within the organization as the Clinical Nurse Educator, but they wanted me to move into a management position to assist my boss in her role running multiple departments.

I wasn't quite sure how to feel. Honestly, I was just trying to sort out the words I had just heard. On one hand, I was in shock. I thought of all the things I had done for the organization: creating a whole new, revenue generating service line, fast-tracking a four-year-long accreditation process to become the fourth hospital in our state to achieve a Global Designation, developing a Nurse Residency Program to decrease staff turnover, not to mention all of the staff training and patient education programs—and they're just "done" with my role?

Then, on the other hand, I was elated because management *was* the next rung on the ladder and was finally within my reach—what an honor! My boss proceeded to tell me that I had the weekend to think about it, but she needed an answer by Tuesday. (It was Labor Day Weekend, and no one would be working on Monday.) No rush, you know . . . just make a quick little decision on something that would change the ENTIRE trajectory of my life in seventy-two hours! (Insert rolling eyes emoji.) The only thing I can remember muttering to her in that moment was, "I'll think about it."

So as I left that day, not sure whether I wanted to skip and cheer or cry to my car, I started thinking about what this new role would mean for my family. Having worked for this organization for more than fifteen years, I knew the ins and outs of most of the "admin" roles. I was thinking to myself, Oh man, this means a new "title" and a raise! I've waited for this for so long! And it also means more time away from my family . . . being on call 24/7/365 . . . getting called in to work on holidays, nights, and weekends when there was a hole in the staffing schedule . . . even after working a forty-plus-hour week.

All of a sudden, this "promotion" opportunity felt more like a death trap! I had three little boys at home; they were a precious gift from God, and I knew I only had a short time with them to do the job that no one else could ever do—be their momma. And that began to tug at my heart.

But what other choice did I have—quit my job?

So, as we always do on Labor Day weekend, my family and I headed to the lake. That entire weekend I fasted and prayed, trying to discern what God wanted me to do. Believe me, I truly felt like I was in labor that weekend! As I wrestled with the decision to be made, Satan took the opportunity to create as much confusion and fear as possible. He gave me thoughts like *Are you really going to throw your career away? What kind of mother would put her children at risk . . . no income, no insurance, no retirement? You're going to lose your home, and your children are going to starve. Your children are going to hate you. Do you really think your marriage is strong enough to handle this?*

The whole time I heard God saying, "You get to choose. You can choose prestige, the 'safety and security' of a job or you can choose to step out in faith and follow me. You can learn to depend on me and watch what I will do."

Let me tell you, that weekend was EXCRUCIATING! Seconds felt like hours, and every decision felt like it was life or death.

But I knew one thing to be true: I wasn't going to let fear rob me of the opportunity to follow God and experience the goodness of what He had in store.

So, with all the courage and faith I could muster, I walked into that hospital Tuesday morning, shaking all the way, and told them I would be resigning my position and would NOT be accepting the offer to move into the management position.

And it felt GOOD! For about five minutes. Then I realized I had to find a way to make money—and fast! But living in a rural area, jobs like mine were practically nonexistent.

I started to think about what I could do. The problem I could solve and how I could help others and earn an income doing it. Then I remembered my training as a coach. I started looking at how to start a coaching business and questioning if this could be a possibility for me.

I discovered that:

- People who were good at social media taught others how to do social media.

- People who were good at fitness taught others how to get healthy and lose weight.

- People who were good at public speaking taught others how to get good at public speaking.

And that's when I realized . . . you can turn your expertise into income.

But what was my expertise?

As I thought about it, it hit me! My expertise is helping others turn their expertise into income by creating coaching programs, training programs, information products, and online courses that could help them make more money, help more people, and make an even bigger impact in the world!

Since that time, I've been able to build a business that allows me to do the things that are most important to me, all while helping others to make a bigger impact in the lives of those they are called to serve.

But it never would have been possible if I had chosen comfort and security over stepping out in faith to do what felt like the impossible. And I'm here to tell you: you can do it too. Whatever that big, scary thing is that you've been called to do, choose to say "yes" to walking in faith—and see what God will do!

Natalie Lavelock, the visionary force behind Natalie Lavelock Coaching & Consulting and The Spirit-Led Entrepreneur, is a dynamic leader in the spiritual arena of business. Since founding her faith-based coaching and consulting firm in 2016, she has risen as a commanding presence, driving clients to achieve extraordinary annual revenues, consistently reaching five, six, and seven figures.

natalielavelock.com

PUSHED OFF THE CLIFF: MY LEAP INTO A LIFE OF JOY AND FULFILLMENT

Lori McDowell, PhD

I wake up and look at the clock. It's 4:45 a.m. I know I should stay in bed and get another hour of sleep, and I can't. I'm not tired. I'm excited to start this beautiful new day.

When I was walking my dog Roxie last night before bed, my mind was writing—it was thinking about the stories I want to tell, the messages I want share, and this morning I can't wait to get them on paper. Loving what you do so much that the need to get started is more important than the need for more sleep is an amazing feeling.

Yet not too long ago, I hated to get out of bed in the morning. I used to set my alarm clock, and when it went off, I'd hit the snooze button three or four times, finally dragging myself out of bed when I couldn't delay any longer. I set the clock twenty minutes fast just to make sure I wouldn't be late. Getting up was a drag, and I had no enthusiasm for the day to come.

Can you be generally happy yet completely lost at the same time? Can you be successful and still feel empty inside? That's exactly how I felt—happy without joy. Successful yet not fulfilled. Content and longing for more.

These were my beliefs:

- I believe life is a joyful place full of possibilities.

- I believe life should be lived to the fullest.

- I believe a fulfilling, joyful life is our birthright.

Why wasn't I living my beliefs?

MY TURNING POINT

I have a PhD in chemical engineering, which means I'm pretty smart when it comes to academics. I had a lot to learn about life.

Today, I do work that I love as a bestselling author, an international, award-winning speaker, and a reinvention coach. I help women like me change their lives, find their joy, and live their dreams. My motto is "Life is meant to be lived, one crazy adventure at a time," and my mission is "to make the world a more joyful place"—and I live by both of these on a daily basis.

I love to travel and have been to forty-seven of the fifty US states and more than forty countries. A drive through Nebraska, South Dakota, and North Dakota is on my bucket list. I love the outdoors. I love sports and competition, both watching and participating, especially baseball, and I'm a huge Houston Astros fan.

My life is shared with my husband, Frank, my son, Hunter, and my dog, Roxie. Health and fitness are important to me, and I try to exercise daily.

I love supporting nonprofits, and I even went so far as to jump off a thirty-story hotel to raise money for one.

So today, my life is pretty great. I'm in the driver's seat. My work is fulfilling and I get satisfaction from seeing my clients get results. I have the time to spend with my family and friends and to do what I love. I jump out of bed every morning looking forward to a new day.

It wasn't always this way . . .

I had spent more than thirty years in corporate America with a big salary, a company car, a paid vacation, healthcare, travel, and an annual bonus. I had the dream that everyone aspires to have—a nice house, fancy car, husband, son, dog. I was a success.

Every job I had always started off great. I would be excited, get amazing results, and be a top performer. Then I'd realize this wasn't enough. The job would become routine and boring, and I'd look for a new position. This cycle usually took about seven years.

Most recently, I worked as director of business development, where I handled multimillion-dollar deals on a regular basis. I had been at this job for about ten years and was still in the content stage. I figured I would work there until I turned sixty-two and my son graduated from college, and then I would retire and do something meaningful.

Life had other plans, however. My boss retired, and a new guy took over. He was a micromanager, and his values and vision for the business were very different than mine. I became frustrated, angry, and stressed, and I hated going to work every day. I wasn't happy, but the pay was good, the job was easy and comfortable, and I thought I could outlast him and get by for a few more years. Then, on April 4, 2023, things went from bad to worse.

My company had a two-day sales meeting in Austin, Texas, about four hours from my home outside Houston. I had some meetings in the morning, then left my house around noon to drive to the hotel, arriving around 4:00 p.m. When I tried to check into my room, the front desk clerk told me my room had been canceled. One of my coworkers was checking in at the same time, and he joked, "That's how they tell you you're fired." We had good chuckle, and the hotel reinstated my reservation.

My boss and I had a meeting scheduled for 4:30 p.m. that afternoon. We had been on a call with a large client that morning, and he told me he wanted to review some things. When I entered the conference room, there was another VP in the room, and a cell phone was sitting on the table. My intuition kicked in. Something wasn't right.

As I sat at the table, a voice on the phone said, "This is Angie from HR. We are terminating your employment. You will be paid until the end of the day." *WHAT? Did I just hear that right? You're firing me and paying me until the end of the day? Did you really make me drive four hours to fire me? I mean who does that?* I was shocked, angry, confused. *How could this happen? Do I yell, cry or punch someone, throw up?*

My emotions were in turmoil. I was angry, terrified, and embarrassed. What would people think? I could just hear the conversations at the sales meeting. "Where's Lori? I saw her at the hotel. Did she get fired?"

I was a mess. How was I going to support my family? What should I do next? I couldn't believe this had happened. How could they do this to me? I was the top salesperson, had the biggest clients, brought in the most revenue.

This can't be real, I thought. And I still had to make that long drive back home.

As I drove home, in rush hour traffic, my imagination conjured up all the horrible outcomes: not finding another job, unable to pay the bills, telling my son he had to withdraw from college, selling the house, moving in with my mom. I was making myself sick. I was about to turn sixty years old, and I felt like a huge failure.

Then suddenly, about halfway home, a thought popped into my head: "I don't have to go to work tomorrow." I felt lighter, joyful, free.

Right then, I decided that I would never again put my success or my joy in someone else's hands. Control of my life belonged to *me*. I realized I had a choice about what I would do next, and I would consciously make that choice, living life on my terms. I reinvented myself during that drive, and everything became clear. Being fired was a gift.

I had spent my life climbing the mountain of success, never asking myself where I was trying to get to. I just kept climbing, and every time I got to the top of a peak, it wasn't where I wanted to be. I switched to a different path and kept climbing.

In this last job, I got higher than I ever had before. I was standing on the top of this mountain, looking down at the beautiful blue water—and *that's* where I really wanted to be. I knew it in my soul. I was too scared to jump.

Then losing my job pushed me off that cliff. Now I'd get to swim in that beautiful blue water!

I wrote a book, *The Reinvention Mindset*. Reimagine U Strategies was created, and my new coaching business took off. Speaking became a priority; I knew my message needed to be shared.

During that long drive home, I learned that we all have the power to take control of our lives. We can make the choice to live the life we desire. We can jump off that cliff. My mission is to help as many people as I can to make that jump.

You don't have to be scared. You don't have to wait for a push, like I did. You can take control of your life and jump off the cliff. You can swim in the beautiful blue water. You can have a life full of joy. You can find success in your soul. All of it is possible. It is a choice—and the choice is yours. And I know you can do it.

Lori McDowell, PhD, is CEO of Reimagine U Strategies and author of *The Reinvention Mindset*. Love and joy are cornerstones of Lori's business. She is a mindset coach, helping high-achieving women find joy and fulfillment in business and life. Lori believes we live our purpose when we embrace our authentic self.

reimagineu.net

SIX MONTHS TO LIVE

Monica Munro

On September 14, 2008, while reading a book, I came across an exercise called "Six Months to Live." If I knew I only had six months to live, what would I be doing? Where would I be living? Who would I be with? What would I change? What would I add? What would I eliminate?

Five days later while reading another book, the same "Six Months to Live" exercise was in it too. Synchronicity!

I did the exercise, recording my answers in a journal. One of those answers was to record my album.

For thirty-three years, I'd had a childhood dream of recording an album, and for thirty-three years, I let a number of reasons (a.k.a. excuses) stop me from pursuing my dream. Two of the big ones were that I didn't have the money, and I didn't know how.

Two months later, I was in Los Angeles for a conference, and there I had the idea of preselling my album. I went up to twelve random people, shared my dream, told them I'd have the album to them in six months to a year, and asked them to pre-buy it. Eleven of the twelve gave me twenty dollars, along with their name and address.

Whoa! I had made it official. It was no longer a private, personal commitment that I could let myself off the hook for if it got challenging. I had made a commitment to eleven people, as well as myself. There could be no more excuses—only results. I now had $220 of the thousands of dollars I imagined I would need, I still didn't know the first thing about recording an album, and now I was committed to figuring it all out. It was scary and exhilarating at the same time!

Five months passed. I made some progress. Nothing substantial though.

On April 6, 2009, I watched the Canadian movie *One Week*, written by Michael McGowan. I was reminded once again of how fleeting life is. The monologue at the end basically asked the same questions as the Six Months to Live exercise had.

I was emotionally moved, and something shifted in me. I was all in. The following quote, by William Hutchison Murray, describes perfectly what happened over the next seven months.

Until one is committed, there is hesitancy, the chance to draw back, always ineffectiveness. . . . The moment one definitely commits oneself, then providence moves too. . . . Whatever you can do or dream you can, begin it. Boldness has genius, power and magic in it. Begin it now.

I talked about my dream to everyone who would listen. One Saturday night, I went to listen to a band playing in town. I ended up talking to the guitar player for a while afterward. He invited me to his next gig in the city, so I went the following week. There I met Ron A. McNeill, a singer/songwriter who had songs getting radio play. I told him about my dream, and he said, "Let's write a hit song together." So we did!

When I met the guitar player's father on another occasion, and told him my dream, he played a song for me that I really liked. I ended up connecting with the songwriter to see about recording it on my album, and he kept asking me who my producer was. Producer? What's a producer? Remember, I didn't know anything about recording an album. So I contacted a keyboardist I had heard about and asked him about the role of a producer, and after telling me, he gave me the contact information of a producer he knew. I met with the producer, and he seemed to know what he was talking about, so I was planning to hire him.

When talking with Ron though, he told me not to make any decision until I met with Rick Mizzoni, an incredible producer he knew. Ron set up a time for the three of us to meet. Even though Rick told us that he wasn't planning on working with anyone else, after listening to my demo tape, he decided to produce my album.

Rick knew and worked with some of the best musicians in Canada, so he put together an ensemble of brilliant musicians for the album. The whole process ended up being so easy! I didn't actually need to know much at all about the process of recording an album. It was simply a matter of making a decision and fully committing, taking the actions in faith, and watching it magnificently unfold.

So, what about the money?

At a networking event I attended, I shared my album story with a lady and my need to find the money to record the album. She gave me one hundred dollars for five albums and told me about an organization she was involved with that offered training on raising capital. I joined the organization, went through the training, and put a script together.

I had taken a nine-month hiatus from entrepreneurship while working on the album, so I asked a guy at work if I could practice my script on him. He said, "Sure." When the time came, he forgot about our scheduled meeting and was heading out the door. I garnered the courage to ask him if I could still practice my script on him. He obliged, came back, and sat down. My boss saw me stumbling through the script and stood there laughing at me. Those awkward ninety seconds felt like an eternity. When I finished, the guy got up without saying a word and left. That was Wednesday night.

Three days later, on Saturday, his day off, this same guy came back to work with his check book. He wrote me a check for six thousand dollars. Unbeknownst to him, it was the exact amount I needed to pay the musicians who were booked two days later to begin recording the album. I was blown away. I'm so glad I didn't let those ninety seconds of feeling pain, humiliation, and rejection stop me from going after my dream.

In the end, I raised the forty-five thousand dollars I needed to complete the album and manufacture one thousand CDs.

One of the most memorable and emotional experiences of my life was being in the recording studio with Rick and my mom, hearing two of the finished songs play. Wow! It was wild! I was listening to my thirty-three-year-old dream being fulfilled with tears streaming down my face.

Mike, the guy at work and first check-writer for my album dream, became my honey, and we've now been together for fifteen years.

That first dream of recording an album led to my second dream of going platinum in Canada (which means selling eighty thousand albums). So far, sales are almost one-sixth of the way to platinum. There's no time limit to reach this goal, so this dream is still alive —just not a current focus.

In the six years after the album was released, for one to three hours a night I knocked on more than 300,000 doors, selling just over fourteen thousand albums, one beautiful conversation at a time. Gross sales of the album were over a quarter of a million dollars (approximately $275,000) during those six years.

Receiving emails, calls, and notes from people around the world whose lives were touched and somehow positively and meaningfully impacted through the album were always highlights of my days. The concerts, the experiences, the learnings, the challenges, the growth . . . the journey. I'm thankful for it all. For all the people who were part of it and who contributed to making it happen . . . for the person I have become as a result of making the decision, committing to it, and following through.

What if I hadn't reflected on my life by doing the Six Months to Live exercise? What if I didn't decide to commit to fulfilling my childhood dream in 2008? What would my life be like now? Would I still have an unfulfilled childhood dream, forty-nine years later? Would I still be living by excuses, not doing the things I'm here to do? Would the people's whose lives were touched and inspired by sharing my dream and story and sharing a conversation with them have been inspired by someone else? Would their lives still have been changed? Would the ripple effect of those changes have happened in the lives they touch?

So, let me ask you: What is stopping you?

- From fulfilling your dreams and your purpose

- From doing what you were put on this earth to do

- From making a difference in people's lives and in the world

The person you become by stepping out of your comfort zone and fulfilling your dreams by eliminating the excuses you've allowed to hold you back—this is the person who will impress you, who you'll feel good about, knowing you've stepped out in faith, said yes to your purpose, and made the difference you are here to make.

We have been given only so many heartbeats in our lifetime. We have no idea how much time we have left. We are not guaranteed even the next second.

Make every moment count.

Monica Munro is a dynamic artist, singer, speaker, author, and Dream Coach. Through her proprietary system, she empowers individuals to align with their God-given purpose, break through limitations, and realize their biggest dreams. Monica inspires others to live boldly, achieve their full potential, and make a meaningful, lasting difference in the world around them.

monicamunro.com

SLEEP WELL, BE WELL

Jennifer Patenaude

I have to say, my life is pretty great these days. Professionally, it's my "second chapter" so to speak. After years of working for others, I'm finally my own boss as an entrepreneur with control over my schedule and who I work with, and I'm genuinely helping people. I'm thankful for my health in allowing me to live this life; I have even, consistent energy during the day, I sleep well at night, and I'm able to take daily stressors in stride.

My time freedom allows me to schedule my work around my kids' high school and college games and events (we're a big lacrosse family). And even though they're both technically adults now and fairly self-sufficient, they still need their mom. They're not completely off the books yet!

It also let me spend significant time with my dad during the nine months prior to his passing. His health struggles required a move into a care facility an hour's drive from me. Thankfully, I was able to visit him often without the guilt of missing work commitments or "punching the clock." For those visits I will be forever grateful.

Even more, I think one of the best parts of being an entrepreneur and building this incredible business is setting an example for my kids of what's possible.

But it wasn't always this way.

In the winter of 2007, I was diagnosed with an autoimmune disease, Sjogren's Syndrome. (Try saying that five times fast.) I didn't know what the heck was going on with me—I thought my whole head was going to shrivel up, it was so dry. Did someone shop-vac all the moisture out while I was sleeping? My eyes felt like someone was rubbing them with sandpaper. If I didn't wash it down with liquid, food would get stuck at the top of my throat.

I even went to the emergency room at one point because both sides of my face along my jawline completely swelled up. I had flashbacks to getting my wisdom teeth removed when I was eighteen. With a bemused look, the ER doctor said I was an "interesting case." Thanks, Doc. Super helpful.

When I finally received the diagnosis, it was a huge relief. But that relief was quickly snatched away when I was told it's a chronic disease that can never be cured and may progress. Oh, and by the way, you'll need to take these medications for THE. REST. OF. YOUR. LIFE.

That was not okay.

In that moment, I felt broken and thought, *What did I do? Why is this happening to me? I have two young children at home and a career, and suddenly my future is so uncertain.*

But I didn't have time for self-pity. My symptoms were manageable, and there was no need to make any major disruptions to my life. Sure, I was fatigued, but with two toddlers and a full-time job, I didn't have the bandwidth to worry about it. I was worrying about daycare and deadlines. My kids' well-being was front and center. So I just took the meds and kept on going.

I adapted. I managed. I certainly wasn't thriving, though.

Fast-forward to January 2020: I learned I could do something about it. When I was introduced to the world of health coaching, there was suddenly this light at the end of the tunnel. *Wait*, I thought, *there are alternatives to the traditional medical system we unquestioningly follow?* Absolutely. Don't get me wrong, our system is the best in the world for certain things, but it's woefully inept at others, such as everyday wellness. I wanted to learn all I could, and that led to my decision to become a health coach.

When I started studying to become a health coach, I was like a kid who just won a golden ticket to Willy Wonka's chocolate factory. The prospect of healing myself and helping others heal felt life-changing.

And, in fact, I had to start putting into practice what I was learning a few months later.

I had this silly kitchen mishap and cut my finger. It turns out that it wasn't so silly after all, because I was already compromised. I end up on two separate courses of antibiotics followed by a bunch of unpleasant symptoms, including visible skin rashes and irritation. I couldn't wear nontoxic (health coach, remember) deodorant for weeks!

But I knew from my health coach training that the traditional medical system wasn't going to be able to truly help me. No thank you to more antibiotics, and forget topical steroid creams. I was going to need to figure this one out on my own. I knew I had to do something different so I could take care of myself. Have you ever felt that way? It only took me thirteen years.

I had a hunch about what was going on, did some research, and made some significant changes to my nutrition and lifestyle.

I made simple changes—not necessarily easy, but simple. Within a week, my symptoms started to disappear. Rashes gone. Welcome back, deodorant! Within two weeks, I had even energy throughout the day and was feeling great.

But when I looked around, I noticed that other people making similar changes weren't getting similar results. And I realized the missing piece of the puzzle was something I already had in place: sleep. That was one of the things I actually got right on this autoimmune carnival ride—listening to my body when it was tired. But even the "healthiest" among us need proper sleep.

You can be the cleanest eater on the planet, do seven HIIT workouts a week, alternate between cold plunges and the sauna (or the wellness trend du jour) all you want. But if you are not getting proper sleep, you CANNOT thrive in health.

It has become my mission to put you to sleep!

So you can take control of your health.

So you can enjoy the people and things that matter most to you.

So you can finally find something that works.

If you struggle with sleep, you may feel like you've tried everything under the sun to fix it. But trying different things for a of couple days at a time every few months is not a winning strategy. Unfortunately, as with most healing, it takes time and a little bit of spaghetti thrown at the wall to see what sticks.

However, there are fundamental areas you can focus on to set yourself up for success: sleep environment, sleep routine, and sleep story.

SLEEP ENVIRONMENT

The physical space where you sleep is the easiest of the three areas to optimize because it's primarily making changes to your space one time. Set it and forget it. For instance, your space is ideally pitch black, as dark as possible. Get rid of all those sneaky light sources like gadgets, cable boxes, digital alarm clocks, or light creeping in from outside. Also, keep the ambient room temperature cool, between sixty and sixty-eight degrees. Our core body temperatures drop in the evening, and a warm room can disrupt sleep.

SLEEP ROUTINE

There's a saying I love: "How well we rise is how well we rest." It may seem counterintuitive, but your sleep routine starts the moment you wake up in the morning. What you do first thing can absolutely impact how well you sleep that night. Getting outside into natural light, without glasses and even on cloudy or rainy days, offers a gradual rise in cortisol and gives you an alert, awake feeling. It also sets an internal timer so your body knows that so many hours later it's time to start decreasing cortisol and increasing melatonin. If the first thing your eyes focus on in the morning is your phone, you're spiking your cortisol, which is a stress response. Not the best way to start your day.

SLEEP STORY

Thirdly, but maybe most importantly, is your sleep story— what's going on inside your head that's getting in the way. We all have stories about most aspects of our lives—relationships, self-worth, various competencies, etc. Often these stories are negative. The same goes for sleep. Have you ever said or heard someone say something along the lines of "I'm a terrible sleeper, always have been"? Physiologically, our cells respond to our thoughts as though they're reality. If you keep playing that story over and over, guess what? That's your reality.

The good news is that stories can be rewritten. When you're in that state between wakefulness and sleep, your brain is vulnerable to suggestion and reprogramming. Try repeating positive, first-person statements like "I'm safe and comfortable in my bed"; "I consistently sleep eight hours a night without interruption"; or "I always wake up feeling rested, refreshed, and ready to start the day."

With all of these suggestions, consistency is key, especially if you've struggled with sleep for a long time. It will take some time to reset your sleep-wake cycle, but the small daily positive shifts will motivate you to keep going.

Rest well and rise brightly.

Jennifer Patenaude, founder of Jennifer Eve Wellness, is a sleep and wellness coach. A graduate of the Institute of Integrated Nutrition, Jen is a student at the School of Applied Functional Medicine and pursuing a certification in Sleep, Stress Management, and Recovery from Precision Nutrition.

jenniferevewellness.com

OUT OF THE ASHES—DON'T CHOOSE TO BE ALONE

Brian Seim

Life is abundant. I'm making an impact.

I'm a Life Champion. I help people find freedom to create Kingdom AI—abundance and impact.

Outside of being a Life Champion, I take my lovely wife out for date night every week . . . without our technology. We get away from the kids a couple of weekends and a week each year. Intimate time for just us.

I take the kids out to the bus every morning and meet them there after school every day. I play with them a couple of times every week: board games, biking through the woods, crafting a Mother's Day gift, or even cooking a meal together. My daughter earnestly asks at the end of most weeks, "What's our adventure this weekend?"

I take the kids on daddy dates regularly—even the ones who are "adulting" and have moved out on their own.

Wife and kids and me. . . I take time for me. I plan time for me. I get out on the lake. In the Twin Ports area, "The Lake" means something: Lake Superior is the largest lake in the world. I get out on the lake to race sailboats in the sunset. I blend my technology skills with crafting by spending time at the local maker space. I get away for a weekend each year to be with God and allow him to work in me and on me. I connect with people at work and in the community—*really* connect. They have my attention, and I have theirs. Everyone is seeking a genuine heartfelt connection while being terrified to make one. I choose to make them and that makes my life more abundant and impactful.

Did I mention that life is great?

FLASHBACK

Well, it wasn't always this way. . . . Growing up, I went to church, I tithed, I was an Eagle Scout, I got good grades with little to no effort. I was a bit of a class clown . . . except when my mom came in as the substitute teacher. That turned me into a shy little mouse.

Church for me was: Praise Brian, almighty Brian—"Brian, you're amazing," "Brian, will you be on the church board?", "Wow, you're in the adult choir." Me, me, me, me! I'm *soooo* special.

I went to college and tried attending another church. You know what I found there? Nothing. Nobody was saying, "Brian, you're *fill in the blank with something wonderful.*" I only visited a few times and then went to find my praise and blow up my ego elsewhere. Somewhere where I might say, "Look at me," and people would look.

Praise me because I'm the greatest, I know everything, everyone thinks the way I do. I was a perfectionist. I was . . . alone. Sure, I wanted people to look at me but not at all of me. I only wanted them to look at the "WOW," "Spectacular," "Outstanding" me. The social media me. The "Hey, you've really got it all together" me.

I worked so hard to be visibly invisible. I just wanted to hear, "You're OK; we like you." Or even a genuine "You're wonderful." I thought that was all I needed.

I was so far away from God . . . but somehow, I said a prayer, more than once. It was arrogant and deluded, but it was simple: "God, just take away this sex addiction, and I'll be the perfect ski racing coach." I repeated it. I was looking for a magic trick, an effortless transformation, a new me with no addictions . . .perfect. Just cut me open and remove the sexuality, the abuse, the offenses, and stitch together the masks of perfection into one coherent me, just the way I imagine myself. Remove my urges, temptations, challenges, pains. Leave me with immense joy and happiness.

The answer to that prayer was a two-by-four across the head. I got caught in my addiction. I lost my job. I was exposed. I did some time. My secret was out. The "rest" of me exposed. I was ready to die. My prayer was answered, at least the part I asked for—just not in the way I described.

I was still disconnected, alone, isolated. I still knew everything, and no one, including God, could accept the reset of me, the invisible me: the one who was sexually active at age five through abuse, the one who struggled with sexual addiction and offense, the one who was not perfect. Me, the broken one.

I was still praying, but it was more like the "grant me suicide by someone else's action" kind of prayer. Then someone showed me the way to salvation and eternal life. Sign me up. I was ready to check in.

I began therapy, started recovery, and joined Celebrate Recovery, a Christ based twelve-step program. I started to connect and belong. I realized I didn't know everything. I discovered that you don't think the way I think. I got "better" in community with God's people, real people. I found that there were people who could know the entire me and still love me and think I'm great. I found people that showed me that God completely, head over heels, loves me. I found peace and joy with people seeking complete reality.

From there, I launched a mastermind group, and shortly after that, I joined another. I learned that recovery is looking back and reliving the past, but a mastermind group, accountability partners, and a coach is imagining and creating a future. I began to sort out the gifts, strengths, and abilities I learned from creating my masks and covering up my addictions and learned how to detach them from the pain, sorrow, loneliness and sadness of living alone in my addiction. I couldn't do it alone. I did it with community, accountability groups, masterminds, and multiple coaches.

One of my mentors, Aaron Walker, says, "Isolation is the enemy." As true as that is, I didn't even realize I was isolated. I was surrounded by people looking to me, listening to me, and following my directions, but I had to keep them at arm's length.

This journey has showed me the way out. I learned that connected, transparent people can create amazing lives and value. Together we create God's Kingdom on earth. God is amazing and will join us and contribute to our creation. His creation.

TODAY

I work as a software engineer to feed my family, but I'm also a hero on a mission. Through my Kingdom Family Leader Mastermind groups, I'm helping Christian men create abundance and impact through blessing themselves, expanding their territory, and serving His Kingdom. Starting with the Kingdom Family Leaders as a launching point, my larger vision is that everyone needs a mastermind. *You* need a mastermind!

If you're not familiar with what a mastermind is, my favorite definition comes from Aaron Walker and Tom Schwab: "A mastermind refers to a group of highly motivated individuals who meet to encourage, challenge, and assist one another." It's not coaching. It's not catching up over coffee. It's not I'm OK; you're OK. It's a genuine community of people who come together to lay down their defenses, come to reality, and speak into one another's lives to create abundance and impact. And that's my mission: helping everyone break through limiting beliefs, set a vision that exceeds their wildest dreams, and take action to get there through personal growth, expanding boundaries, and building His Kingdom.

FOR YOU

1. Bless yourself: Nurture your mind, body, and soul. Treasure yourself, your whole self. Know that whatever you've done, wherever you've been, whatever has happened to you, God can use it for good (see Romans 8:28). Forgive yourself, forgive others, forgive God. Know yourself and set forth your mission, vision, and values. Love and bless yourself.

2. Expand your territory: Knowing yourself starts by connecting with REAL people. There is someone in your life that is ready for REALity; they're just waiting for your invitation. I want connection, and you want connection. Others are just as terrified about connection as you are, and if you reach out you'll probably be surprised. Build community, generate accountability, create a mastermind and . . .

3. Build His Kingdom (change the world): Close your eyes and imagine a better world, a world without all the bad stuff you went through, a world of reality and truth. Use your territory to make one baby step toward that better world. Change your thinking; change your actions. Do something new.

Rinse and repeat.

You be blessed!

As a Christian, husband, father, and stepfather of five, **Brian Seim** is the founder of Kingdom Family Leaders Mastermind. He believes that isolation is a barrier to personal growth and fulfillment. "You Need a Mastermind" is his mission to get everyone in the world into a mastermind group.

https://brianseim.com

HIGH-VIBE HEALING TECHNIQUES

Leah Seim

If you can see the invisible, you can achieve the impossible.

—Frank Gaines

What's the best way to move beyond chronic pain, depression, and feeling dog-tired every day between brunch and sundown? I believe it's by raising your energy levels. Why? Because that's what helped me take back my health after a horrible incident broke me back in 2019.

It all started when my hubby and I left Colorado city life to move back to Minnesota. We would be closer to family, especially my parents, and childhood friends. We found the perfect house near Lake Superior, nestled in the woods. It was big, red, and close enough to the great outdoors that we could take our five children and go sailing, skiing, biking, or boating with relative ease. I was looking forward to taking my husky for bike rides on the trails and resuming one of my favorite passions: teaching a few lessons at the local ski area. My husband worked from home, so we thought we had everything we needed when an epic snowstorm shut down Duluth on Black Friday. Well, that is, until our snowblower broke down and we were forced to clear one hundred feet of driveway by hand. After a few hours, I could feel my breath catching painfully in my chest. I'd been dealing with this problem on and off for the past few years, so I wasn't particularly worried—just annoyed.

I defiantly chucked one more shovelful of snow into the teeth of the storm, then stumbled back inside to take an aspirin and check on the kids. However, my heart felt as if it were swelling even more, and suddenly I heard a small popping noise. Next, a rush of blood eased the pain in my chest . . . until I tried to breathe; I felt like a straw had been shoved into my heart. I lurched into the bedroom, asking God to save me before I passed out.

The next few weeks were a blur. I made it to the hospital, where the doctors informed me that I hadn't suffered a heart attack and said I could go back to my life. But once I was back at home, I experienced ongoing pain, fatigue, and brain fog, and I felt barely able to exist moment by moment. Sixteen months later, I begged God to fix me or bring me home because I couldn't stand to live without hope. God started me on my healing path through alternative medicine.

With newfound determination, I jump-started my passion to live my life as a whole person instead of the cracked shell I'd become. It took me years of research, trials, and hindsight before I sorted out most of my issues and formed a plan of action to get back on my feet. I discovered some hard truths and pitfalls along the way that also might help you navigate your own healing journey.

My formula for success goes like this: body times environment times attitude equals a beautiful new you. Start out by evaluating your body and writing down everything you love and hate to eat and why. You can use the first three items off the top of your head or go deep. For instance, one of my favorite foods is home-made waffles because of the comfort and nostalgia of watching my dad make them as a Sunday morning treat as I was growing up. However, if you say you love liver and onions, my gut will squinch together in protest! Why? Because I had issues eating meat products as a kid, and now that I'm older, my body doesn't process meat at all.

So, for your health's sake, think about what you put in your body and how to make it better for you. Personally, I believe adding a scoop of mixed seeds, grains, and nuts will boost anyone's health without too much effort. You can include liquid micro-mineral and vitamin supplements like Ion5 and glutathione to get energy straight into your cells where it's needed. Remember, you know your own body, and you can test out new ways to be healthy.

The next thing you can do for yourself is eliminate any environmental factors that contribute to your condition. Lots of things can affect your energetic body in a positive or negative way. My doctors didn't ask about the possibility of the effects of negative energy from nearby powerlines and our everyday technology, including our cell phones. They didn't mention the negative effects of possible forever chemicals in the water or suggest that we make sure there wasn't mold or radon leaking into the house.

They also didn't mention positive ways to create a healthy space and harmonize the energy around you. I discovered on my own the benefits of using sound therapy techniques, and hanging out under my crystal singing pyramid. I discovered there are crystals, such as shungite, that absorb electronic energy. Other crystals like yellow citrine are purported to help with healing, meditation, and abundance. Each of us can discover what will bring us into higher resonance. If nothing else, I enjoy having various crystals around for their beauty and graceful shapes, and I felt better after buying them.

The last thing you can do to bring up your vibration above chronic pain is through positive thoughts and actions and gentle exercises like stretching and tai chi. I supplement exercise with oxygen to clear any lactic acid buildup. Also, becoming part of a high-energy tribe has helped me cope in a healthier way. As part of my morning routine, I speak out life-giving "I am" statements. I get into the words of God in the Bible. I pray for myself and others. And, during the day, I listen to music at a 432 Hz frequency, which helps me feel good when my energy runs low. Breathwork also has helped me listen to my body and understand how to replenish it.

The people I've met along the way are beautiful souls I asked God to put in my path to help me along the way. Especially when they are super annoying, they challenge me to grow in love, gratitude, and prayer. One of my favorite prayers for this type of person, especially a difficult boss, is "Lord, I know you put this person in my path to help me learn some important lesson, so please help me learn it faster!"

I really don't know how I would have managed to stay alive if I didn't have other people around who were finding their own way through their pain and back to their lives. It was a shock to find out that I wasn't alone, and I didn't have to fight my chronic issues by hiding away under a blanket and a heating pad for untold hours.

Vibrating above your pain starts with believing you are loved and worthy to be healthy and then doing things to make it happen for real. As Zig Zigler wrote in his book *See You at the Top*, "We all need a daily CHECK UP from the neck up to avoid 'stinkin thinkin' which can ultimately lead to hardening of the attitudes. Happiness begins with becoming more aware of the negative thought patterns that entrap us and converting them to positives." You can achieve this on your own; however, I found time and again that it comes faster with friends who understand what you are dealing with and can back you up. There are a lot of online resources you can use to connect with other people. It can be as simple as finding an online prayer group or Bible study. It might be a group session set up by a counselor. If you want a little nudge along the way, I'm here, too. I can help you streamline your path back to your life.

In the meantime, take a breath and look at your amazing life so far. You have done so much more than you know. You have made a difference in people's lives that you don't even remember. And you are ready to face this challenge head on.

Remember: First find any hidden allergies, get liquid supplements, and make healthier food choices. Next, align your environment to your new self by eliminating hazards and equalizing the energy around you and your home. Last, do the therapies and exercises that will help you vibrate above your pain to get back to feeling normal. I believe in you, and I'm hopeful that, unlike me, it won't take years to get back to feeling able to do things you want to do.

Leah Seim is a life and wellness coach, entrepreneur, speaker, and bond servant to God. She has a bachelor's degree in psychology, is married her soulmate, and is a mom of all trades.

leahcall.me

MIRROR MOMENTS: REDISCOVERING CONFIDENCE AT ANY AGE

Katie Sevenants

I believe that when we identify and value our own unique wisdom and experiences, we radiate confidence inside and out.

I believe that we can support one another in business and life when we are inspired by one another rather than comparing and competing.

I believe that we can accomplish more and make a bigger difference in our community when we connect, collaborate, and encourage one another.

I've run a thriving beauty business for twenty-two years. As a certified ELITE Makeup Artist specializing in anti-aging skincare and color theory, I've had the privilege of helping countless women feel beautiful in their own skin.

I feel extremely blessed.

At sixty-one years old, I'm living my best life. I have a close relationship with my adult daughters, I'm a fun loving GiGi (grandma to two and one on the way), and I've been married for thirty-four years. I work my beauty business from home and continue to be in the top 1 percent of my direct sales company. Over the years, I've earned many company incentives, from car lease payments to trips around the world—Costa Rica being my favorite so far (that coffee!). But the best part? I've helped thousands of women feel confident in their own skin.

My husband and I are pretty active. We love to hike, kayak, snowshoe, and play a bit of pickleball . . . doesn't everyone? I'm excited for the future and looking forward to more travel and adventures in the years to come. Living in sunny Colorado, I'm fortunate to be just minutes away from trails where I can escape into nature.

But it wasn't always this way.

In my fifties, I had a pivotal moment I call my "mirror moment." My daughters were off on their own, no longer dependent on me. While I was happy for them, I felt lost and empty. Our goal as moms is to raise strong, independent, happy kids, and I did that! But suddenly, I found myself with a big hole in my heart.

One day, I looked in the mirror, and all I saw was an old woman. The wrinkles around my eyes seemed deeper, and gray strands that once peeked through were now everywhere. As a makeup artist and anti-aging expert, I spent my days helping women feel beautiful, yet when I looked at myself, I struggled to see beyond the imperfections. I felt a deep sense of uncertainty—a fear of fading relevance in a world that often prizes youth above all else. I found myself staying home more often, not wanting to go anywhere, and being hard on myself and my husband.

The beauty industry, my professional playground for over two decades, seemed to echo my insecurities. Youth was celebrated everywhere I turned, and I couldn't help but question my place. The younger generation was making videos on social media and thriving in my industry, and I began to doubt my value as a business owner. How could I still make a difference when all I saw in the mirror was an aging woman in a fast-paced world? Was I tech-savvy enough to keep up with the rapidly evolving digital landscape? Did I still have what it took to be creative and passionate about my work? Was I too old to learn something new or to con-nect and make an impact anymore? These doubts gnawed at me, threatening to overshadow the confidence I once had.

At times, the weight of these uncertainties felt suffocating. I even considered abandoning my dream—my flourishing business that had afforded me the free-dom to be home while raising my family and still earn an income. The friends and co-workers I respected and enjoyed connecting with. The thousands of loyal customers I had over the years. The thought of giving it all up for a conventional nine-to-five job left me feeling trapped and hopeless, my dreams slipping through my fingers like grains of sand.

I knew something had to change. I had to change. I needed to make money for my family, and I knew I didn't want to give up on my dream life to work for some-one else. It was time to go all in.

Have you ever felt like everything was crumbling down around you?

Somewhere deep within me, a flicker of resilience stirred—a spark that refused to be extinguished. I sought guidance from mentors who helped me realize that the solution wasn't "out there"; it was inside me. I started investing in myself, focusing on my mindset and shifting from self-doubt to self-discovery. I began journaling and visualizing my future life as if it were already happening. I began writing daily in a gratitude journal and started to see the value I brought to the world—value that wasn't dependent on anyone or anything else but me, just as I was.

A tool I used that made a significant impact was creating an inventory of at least twenty things: my accomplishments, my values, my strengths, and the things I liked about myself. One of my mentors calls it "Your List of Awesomeness." I made copies of this list and posted them everywhere: on my mirror, so I could read it every morning; next to my computer screen, so I could remind myself of my qualities before going live; and even on my car visor, so I could read it before heading into a networking event or meeting.

With each passing day, I embraced my journey, celebrating both my triumphs and failures without fear of judgment. I was thoughtful with my words and actions about myself, knowing my girls were paying attention. I started remembering qualities in myself that I had forgotten. I used to push the boundaries of my comfort zone all the time. I didn't just go skydiving once; I did it a second time the same day just so I could enjoy it more—the first jump was a blur... maybe a few seconds of blacking out!

Slowly but surely, I started to show up authentically in my business. I addressed my insecurities with my audience and created a stronger bond with them. I had no idea so many others felt the same. My online community grew—not just to buy products but to connect and share our common feelings and experiences.

In my personal life, I embraced not having all the answers in this new chapter and got excited about what it could look like. My husband and I sought new adventures we could experience for the first time together, like cooking new dishes and traveling to new places. We started getting out every weekend and hiking in the mountains. We learned to kayak, which gave us each the time to reflect and to get creative about our future.

Most importantly, I started to show up confidently in front of that mirror. I learned to see beyond the superficial and embrace the beauty that comes with experience and self-acceptance. My wrinkles became badges of honor, each telling a story of resilience and growth. The gray in my hair became a symbol of wisdom earned through years of navigating life's twists and turns.

My team grew, and I started attracting new clients. Rather than hiding my feelings and emotions behind what I thought was the perfect image, I realized that what I felt was holding me back was exactly what others needed to see and feel to know they weren't alone. I help women who are afraid to show up on camera—women who have stopped taking time for themselves, let alone trying anything new—see the value in investing in themselves. They learn to feel confident in their own skin and then share that with others. I love watching the way small shifts in how we believe in ourselves can give others the permission to do the same. I get excited thinking about the possibilities!

Have you ever felt like your best days are behind you? What if I told you that your greatest moments are still ahead?

Instead of hitting midlife and feeling unworthy, stuck, or lost, you can show up confident and excited about what's next. Instead of focusing on your outer beauty, value what's inside—your unique gifts, your talents, and your experiences. When you realize your true beauty, you will radiate confidence.

One of my favorite ways to end my day now is something I learned in the book *The Magic* by Rhonda Byrne. Find a small rock—any kind, from your yard or a beautiful stone in a gem shop. Pick it up and hold it right before you fall asleep and review your day to find the best thing that happened to you. This process helps you get in the habit of looking for the good in your day instead of focusing on the bad.

I'm living proof that transformation is possible at any age and for anyone. Just like me, you have the power to redefine your life and succeed with confidence. Remember, confidence isn't about being flawless; it's about showing up as your true self, flaws and all.

Katie Sevenants empowers entrepreneurs to radiate confidence on camera and on stage. An international bestselling co-author, dynamic speaker, coach, and mentor in her thriving beauty business, she is also an adventurous wife, mom, and GiGi, with a passion for the outdoors and a fearless spirit that has even included skydiving!

KissMeKatie411.com

THE QUIET DESTRUCTION: HOW IGNORING YOUR INNER VOICE LEADS TO EXTERNAL CHAOS

Glenda Tan

Life today is great, but it hasn't always been this way . . .

There was a time when everything seemed perfect on the outside. I had the career, the income, and the admiration of those around me. People saw me as the epitome of success. But what they didn't see was the war I was waging on two fronts: internally, with feelings of inadequacy and the need to be perfect, and externally, with the constant demands of a life that looked successful but felt deeply unfulfilling.

Mornings began with a racing heartbeat and a sense of dread. The constant travel, endless meetings, and relentless pressure weighed heavily on me. I was trapped in a cycle of anxiety and exhaustion, suffocated by the very life I had worked so hard to create.

Despite my achievements, I felt sadness, frustration, and emptiness. I had been led to believe that career success would naturally bring lasting happiness. Yet I found myself in a cheerless place, constantly at war both internally and externally, and uncertain about what I truly wanted.

Then, on September 25, 2019, everything changed.

I was in London, walking down Pread Street, lost in thoughts about work. I was so absorbed in my worries that I didn't notice the bus until it was too late. *Bam!* It hit me. In that split second, everything stopped. Time seemed to stand still as I realized what had just happened. I should have been seriously injured or worse, but somehow I walked away without a scratch.

That moment was my wake-up call. In that instant, I knew I couldn't continue on the same path. Something deep inside me shifted. I realized that I didn't want to just exist; I wanted to truly live.

Like many of you, I started my journey with self-help books, Google searches, and YouTube videos. I devoured countless books and watched numerous videos, searching for the secret to breaking the code. Each time I thought I had found it, I tried to implement the lessons, only to be disappointed when I ended up back where I started.

As the saying goes, "When the student is ready, the teacher will appear." One day, Bob Proctor, a leading expert featured in *The Secret*, appeared in my email inbox. Since my way wasn't working, I decided to listen to what he had to offer.

Bob Proctor taught that our paradigms—deep-seated beliefs and habits that shape how we see the world and ourselves—control almost every aspect of our lives, from our thoughts to our actions. When our paradigms are rooted in fear, doubt, and limitation, they create barriers between who we are and who we want to become.

But paradigms aren't the only force at play. Our inner self-image—how we see ourselves at our core—is just as powerful. According to *Psycho-Cybernetics* by Dr. Maxwell Maltz, our self-image acts like a thermostat, regulating what we believe we're capable of achieving. If our self-image is low, no amount of external success will feel satisfying because we'll never believe we're truly deserving of it.

For me, my self-image had been shaped by years of playing small, defining myself through my job and the roles I played rather than through my true passions and desires. Deep down, I knew there was more to me than the roles I was playing, but my self-image wouldn't allow me to see it. It kept me confined to a life that, while outwardly successful, was inwardly unfulfilling.

TURNING THE TIDE

To change your life, you must reprogram your paradigms and reshape your self-image. But before you can reconnect with your inner voice and begin living the life you truly desire, you must first face the reality of who you are right now. This requires confronting the stories you've been telling yourself, the roles you've been playing, and the expectations you've been trying to meet. It's about being brutally honest with yourself about whether this is the person you want to be. This honesty is the foundation upon which true transformation is built.

The first step is acknowledging your present state—emotionally, mentally, and spiritually. This can be daunting because it often involves looking at parts of yourself you may have been avoiding. But until you face these aspects head-on, real change will remain out of reach.

Once you've faced the truth of who you are, the next step is to summon the bravery to move forward. This process requires courage, self-reflection, and a willingness to listen to the whispers of your soul—those quiet urgings that have been ignored for too long.

However, to make lasting changes, you must go deeper. You need to reprogram your paradigms and reshape your self-image. Paradigms are the subconscious programming that governs your thoughts, behaviors, and ultimately, the results you achieve in life. These paradigms are like invisible forces that control your decisions and actions, often without your conscious awareness.

Reprogramming these paradigms isn't something you can do alone. Because they are deeply embedded in your subconscious, it requires external support and proven methods to shift them effectively. Think of it as trying to rewire the operating system of your mind—this isn't a task that can be done with willpower alone. It requires a systematic approach and the guidance of someone who understands the process.

This is where the power of mentorship and coaching comes in. A skilled mentor or coach can help you identify the specific paradigms that are holding you back and guide you through the process of reprogramming them. This isn't just about making surface-level changes; it's about getting to the root cause of the problem and addressing it at its source. The method I discovered and now use is based on a rich lineage of nearly ninety years of scientific and psychological research. It's a method that has stood the test of time because it works. It's not just a theory or a quick fix—it's a process that has been developed, refined, and proven to be effective over decades. This method combines the best of scientific understanding with practical psychological techniques, allowing you to make deep and lasting changes to your paradigms and self-image.

You need to start by challenging the beliefs that have been holding you back. Begin to question whether the stories you've been telling yourself—about success, about your worth, about what you're capable of—are really true. Are they your beliefs, or are they someone else's expectations that you've internalized? This is where reprogramming begins—by identifying and dismantling the limiting beliefs that have been controlling your life.

Next, work on creating a new self-image, one that aligns with the life you truly want to live. Your self-image is like a thermostat, regulating what you believe you're capable of achieving. If your self-image is low, no amount of external success will feel satisfying because you'll never believe you're truly deserving of it. Visualize yourself as the person you want to be—someone who is successful but also fulfilled, someone who honors their own needs and desires, someone who lives with purpose and passion. As you begin to see yourself in this new light, your actions and behaviors will start to change.

But remember, this is not a journey you need to undertake alone. Reprogramming your paradigms and reshaping your self-image requires consistent effort, support, and guidance. That's why having a mentor or coach is so crucial. They will provide the accountability, encouragement, and expertise needed to help you navigate this transformation.

THE POWER OF RECONNECTION

Ignoring your inner voice may lead to external chaos, but it's within your power to turn the tide. By first facing the truth of who you are, understanding where you currently stand, and acknowledging your inner needs and desires, you can begin to rebuild the connection with yourself, your loved ones, and your life purpose. This journey isn't about abandoning your professional goals; it's about aligning them with your true self so your success is not just outwardly impressive but deeply fulfilling.

Reconnecting with your inner voice is the key to living a life that is not only successful but also meaningful. It's the foundation upon which true success is built—a success that is sustainable, authentic, and in harmony with your deepest values and aspirations.

The turning point for me was realizing that I didn't have to live according to someone else's script. I had the power to rewrite my story, to create a life that was aligned with my values and my dreams. And so do you.

Your turning point is within reach. It's the moment you decide to take control of your life, listen to your inner voice, and pursue the life you truly want to live. It's the moment you choose to break free from the constraints of your old paradigms and step into the fullness of your potential.

Glenda Tan, a managing director at a multinational corporation and a speaker living in Singapore, is inspired to empower others to master their thoughts, emotions, and environment for a happier, healthier, wealthier life. She uses a ninety-year-old, science-backed framework to help others shatter their internal barriers, and her goal is to build a supportive community in Asia.

linkedin.com/in/glendatan

THREE PILLARS OF PROFIT

Carrie Wallis

I believe you have the right to the help you want when you need it. I believe that you have the skills, knowledge, and experience to make a massive difference in the world. I also believe that when you're free from the shackles of the past that have kept you stuck, you can achieve anything.

Today, I'm blessed. I'm incredibly lucky. My life is amazing. I'm a bestselling author, a speaker, I'm qualified in many streams of coaching, and I've spoken at international conferences. All of this has led to a business that I love. I tell you this to let you know what's possible. I'm privileged to work with the most amazing heart-centered coaches, entrepreneurs, and healers. I get to enjoy three-day weekends where I can enjoy kayaking, bushwalking, and board games. Yes, I'm a Monopoly freak with my husband and my two adult children when they visit. Our ragdoll cat, Captain Jack, rules our house and graciously allows my husband and me and our mini foxy dog to share the space with him.

But it wasn't always like this.

To understand why, I need to take you back in time just a little bit. I left the corporate world at the end of the 1990s when we started our family and I wanted to be an at-home mum. I wanted to do the school runs. I'd been a latchkey kid and

I hated coming home to a cold and empty house, and I didn't want that for my children. So, I started my own business, initially buying into a network marketing franchise. Oh my gosh, not for me—I was really uncomfortable with the sales tactics in that environment.

But I did want to do something. As I had a background in IT, I decided to tap into this knowledge to help solopreneurs navigate the evolving world of the internet to find customers. I was incredibly happy. Our house was full of warmth and love and laughter. It really was blissful until one day everything changed.

My husband was diagnosed with cancer and one short year later he died.

To say I was devastated is a real understatement. I was so frustrated. It was so unfair. Life was cold, empty. I was incredibly lonely. My support had gone. I was lost, confused, and completely overwhelmed. I didn't know which way to turn, or what to do. There was no inheritance for me, and my business, at that time, was little more than a hobby.

I was so desperate to find clients that I was absolutely into the shiny object syndrome. I tried pretty much every marketing strategy there was, with little effect. I simply had to find a way to consistently attract clients and make profit fast or we were going to lose our house and my young children didn't deserve that.

I finally found a mentor and looked at what had been working and what hadn't worked. I threw out all the stuff that hadn't worked. I took a gazillion marketing courses, achieved copywriting qualifications, digital marketing qualifications including Google Analytics, and more.

I built on my experience and figured out a way to consistently attract new clients and generate substantial income that was sustainable, all *without complicated funnels or high tech*. The biggest things I threw out were those sleazy sales and marketing tactics from my network marketing days. What I did keep was the belief that the foundation of marketing is relationships. Genuine relationships.

Through it all, I figured out that there are three secrets to consistently profitable marketing: connection, clarity, and confidence.

CONNECTION

Connection is the human-to-human bond. It's crucial in the age of technology and AI. You see, marketing success comes from the person you are and the relationships you build with your audience. Successful marketing is engaging your audience in conversation, and to do that, they need to feel connected with you.

We humans are a social species. If you struggle to connect with your audience, they will struggle to know you, like you, and trust you. When your message is clear and you can create content that resonates with your audience and shows them you understand their pain, they will feel connected to you and will recognize you as the right person to help them.

There are many ways to connect with your audience. Some of the most effective are stages and podcasts where the audience gets to see and hear you. They know you're a real person, and if you follow the principles of connection they will bond with you.

So, what are the principles of connection? They are understanding, emotion, and consistency. Create each of these in every piece of content you produce—written, visual, and verbal—and your audience will connect with you.

When you connect effectively, you become a client beacon. Without connection, you risk being surrounded by potential clients but unable to reach them.

CLARITY

Clarity is about having a crystal-clear view of the path ahead. You know what to do, how to do it, and you know without a shadow of doubt that what you are doing is right for the person you are. This makes tasks feel effortless and easy to repeat.

Consider Monica, who was generating zero new leads weekly. She was confused and overwhelmed, and she was forcing herself to create Instagram reels despite hating it. Her marketing strategy was all over the place; it was confused and clearly not energizing for her.

Marketing is meant to be fun and energizing, not depleting and exhausting. If you think about it, marketing is like a jigsaw puzzle: There are many pieces that need to fit together, and just as with a jigsaw puzzle, there is a central component to profitable marketing that holds all the other pieces together.

What is that critical piece?

It's your marketing personality. It's identifying what strategy works for the person you are. When you know this, everything else falls into place, feels effortless, and energizes you to consistently take the actions you need.

When Monica completed my marketing personality assessment, she realized where she had been going wrong. We were able to create a strategy specific for her that felt right. She began to enjoy marketing her business and within a month had signed on her first new client in over a year.

Without clarity, you risk wasting time and money, becoming stressed, and potentially wanting to quit. It's crucial to find a marketing approach that feels good for you and aligns with who you are.

CONFIDENCE

Confidence is essential when communicating with your audience. Who enjoys talking with people who are so nervous that the whole conversation feels awkward? Not me. When you're confident in who you are, people are drawn to you.

My own journey with confidence was challenged when I was diagnosed with cancer five years after my husband's death. I feared people wouldn't see me as whole, especially when I lost my hair during chemo. This experience made me realize I had never truly believed I was worthy of success or that I was enough.

This lack of self-belief kept me stuck, preventing me from taking my business to the next level. It stopped me from connecting with my audience effectively. So, while recovering from cancer, I worked on myself; I went deep inside identifying and then releasing the source of my lack of self-worth.

As a result, I changed how I saw myself, which in turn changed how my clients saw me. This led to massive growth in my business, and I was able to take things to a whole new level.

Unshakeable confidence is much more than affirmations or mantras. It's believing deep in your core that you are worth it, you are enough, and you deserve success. When you truly believe you can do it and cannot fail, everything becomes easier, and nothing will get in your way.

I want to quickly distinguish between confidence and arrogance, however. Arrogance is believing you know it all and constantly competing to show how good you are. Confidence, on the other hand, allows you to relax, not make everything about you.

When you have unshakeable confidence you can revel in others' successes, and that's an incredibly attractive quality.

When you radiate confidence:

- Your ideal clients trust you more.
- You know you can't fail despite setbacks.
- You are able to pick yourself faster when setbacks occur.

- You stop questioning and doubting, focusing instead on doing and being.

- You become a beacon for your ideal clients.

- You appear more trustworthy to your audience.

Believe in yourself and ask, "Why not me?" Remember, marketing success comes from the combination of connection, clarity, and confidence. When you master these elements, you'll attract high-quality clients who value your time and expertise.

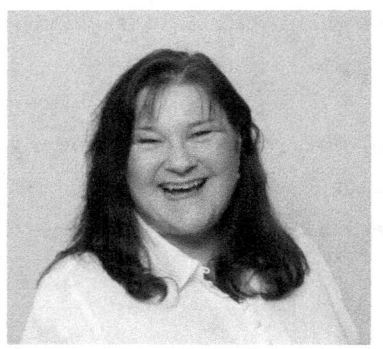

An English woman living in Australia, **Carrie Wallis** is a bestselling author, certified in multiple coaching streams, a qualified copywriter and digital marketer, professional speaker, marketing mentor, and educator. Coaches, healers, and entrepreneurs hire Carrie to help them craft a message that resonates with their audience, engages, and leads to sales.

enlightenusolutions.com

www.ingramcontent.com/pod-product-compliance
Lightning Source LLC
Chambersburg PA
CBHW071208120626
46546CB00006B/2466